SAINT
CATHERINE
OF SIENA

Mystic of Fire

Preacher of Freedom

PAUL MURRAY, OP

WORD ON FIRE
INSTITUTE

Published by the Word on Fire Institute, an imprint of
Word on Fire, Park Ridge, IL 60068
© 2020 by Word on Fire Catholic Ministries
All rights reserved.

23 22 21 20 1 2 3 4

ISBN: 978-1-943243-57-0

Library of Congress Control Number: 2020933631
Murray OP, Paul, 1947–

https://wordonfire.institute

To the memory of Don Briel
(1947–2018)
and
for Colin Howell

The truth will set you free from falsehood. It will dissolve all shadows, giving you light and knowledge in God's mercy. In this truth, you will be freed.
                        —St. Catherine of Siena

Hegel attributed to Christianity the discovery of freedom as the common good of all men and women: this idea was not known to the pre-Christian Orient nor to the Greek world. Freedom came into the world with Christ who taught that all men and women are made in the likeness of God, and so are equal under one common Father.
                        —Cornelio Fabro

. . . freedom, the miracle,
the unnecessitated act.
                        —Eugenio Montale

CONTENTS

ACKNOWLEDGEMENTS

The first public conference I ever gave and the first paper I ever published were on St. Catherine of Siena. With the passage of time, my interest in the life and work of Catherine has remained strong, quickened in no small measure by the work of fellow Dominicans such as Mary O'Driscoll, Suzanne Noffke, Giacinto d'Urso, Kenelm Foster, Mary Ann Fatula, and Thomas McDermott. To them, and to a wide range of other commentators on St. Catherine, I am greatly indebted. I want also to thank in a most particular way John B. Martino for the kind and thoughtful attention he gave to this work at a particular stage, and also to Ben McGuire for his very detailed and scrupulous reading of the text. I am also indebted to three Dominican friends, Robert Ombres, Philip McShane, and Vivian Boland, for devoted and timely consideration of the work, and to Luanne Zurlo, Alexander C. Erikson, Sister Katherine Elena Wolff, Fernando Cervantes, and Andrew Bowie for practical help and encouragement. Lastly, I wish to express my gratitude for the hospitality received, over the long period of research and writing, from the Dominican communities of Tallaght, Cambridge, and Oxford.

Parts of the present work appeared in "Catherine of Siena: The Saint of Our Humanity," *Chicago Studies* (Spring 1999): 60–71, and in a short chapter, "On Fire with Truth: The Life and Teaching of St. Catherine of Siena," *CATHOLICISM: The Pivotal Players, Study Guide*, vol. 1, ed. Robert Barron (Word on Fire Catholic Ministries, 2016).

With regard to the translation of St. Catherine's work: when not otherwise indicated, the translation is my own. Mostly, however, I have relied on translations of the *Dialogue*, *Letters*, and *Prayers* by Suzanne Noffke. (Of great value to scholars, it's worth noting here, are the detailed editorial notes that accompany all three of the Noffke translations.) On rare occasions, I have used the translations of Vida D. Scudder (*Saint Catherine as Seen in Her Letters* [London: Dent, 1927]), and Kenelm Foster and Mary John Ronayne (*I, Catherine* [London: Collins, 1980]). The Italian edition of Catherine's letters, in six volumes, was published in 1940 in Florence under the care of Piero Misciattelli, with notes by Niccolò Tommasèo.

INTRODUCTION
Catherine's Living Voice

The writings of Catherine of Siena have come down to us from a period of history remote from our own. And yet this young, medieval laywoman[1] is able to speak to us today with compelling authority. The enormous distance in time between her world and ours in no way diminishes the impact of her teaching. She remains alive in her great work *The Dialogue*, which presents a series of exchanges between God the Father and Catherine about the spiritual life, and also in *The Prayers*, which she dictated while in ecstasy in the presence of her friends and disciples. But the place where Catherine survives with most immediacy and impact is in her *Letters*, writing at times with the warmth and loving audacity of a girl-child or a mother, and at other times with all the power and passion of an Old Testament prophet: "Let it not seem hard to you if I pierce you with the words which the love of your salvation has made me write; rather would I pierce you with my living voice, did God permit me."[2]

Like any other theologian, Catherine, in her writings, presents and explores the great truths of the Christian faith. Her teaching, however, tends to assume the form of ardent exhortation rather than dogged and detailed exposition. She is clearly not a scholastic

---

1. The designation of Catherine as "laywoman" is probably the most accurate way of describing her status. She was certainly not a religious nun. Most of her life she spent at home with her family. At a certain stage, however, while still remaining at home, she became a member of a group of women in Siena called the *Mantellate*. These were secular Tertiaries, mostly widows, who enjoyed a close connection with the Dominican order.

2. Catherine of Siena, Letter to Three Italian Cardinals, T 310, trans. Vida D. Scudder, *Selected Letters of Caterina Benincasa: Saint Catherine of Siena as Seen in Her Letters* (London: J.M. Dent & Co., 1905), 283.

theologian. For all her brilliance, Catherine comes across to us more as an apostle than an intellectual, more as a preacher than a scholar. If we are to think of Catherine in relation to a text like the *Summa theologiae* of St. Thomas Aquinas, her work, we can say, is like a *Summa* set on fire, her writings characterized not by academic speculation but rather by a passionate and anguished concern for the salvation of the world.

Most studies on Catherine refer at some point to the freedom of speech and action she enjoyed as a young woman, her courage and her boldness. But up to now the uniquely focused attention on freedom in Catherine's work, her sharp and clear understanding of the path to freedom, has received surprisingly little attention from readers and scholars.[3] One of the main aims of the present work is to demonstrate that a preoccupation with freedom—a passionate concern to liberate others from bondage—is the "fire" behind almost every page and paragraph she writes. It is what distinguishes her as an apostle and theologian.

Catherine cajoles, she pleads, she encourages, she bullies, and she inspires. Though concerned first and last with truth, she

---

3. There is, however, one important article on the subject by Cornelio Fabro, "Mutuo accrescimento di libertà e grazia secondo S. Caterina," in *Nuovi Studi Cateriniani*, no. 984, *Supplemento Annuale alla Rivista di Ascetica e Mistica* (Siena: Dominican Roman Province of St. Catherine of Siena, 1984), 54–65. An earlier version of this article, entitled "Libertà e grazia in S. Caterina," was published in *Rivista di Vita Spirituale* 1 (1981): 79–99. Worth noting also is a brief illuminating reflection by Matthew Levering on Catherine's understanding of predestination and freedom in *Predestination: Biblical and Theological Paths* (Oxford: Oxford University Press, 2011), 90–95. Grazia Mangano Ragazzi comments at one point on the subject of freedom, connecting it with St. Catherine's teaching on "holy discretion" in *Obeying the Truth: Discretion in the Spiritual Writings of Saint Catherine of Siena* (Oxford: Oxford University Press, 2014), 188–189. Other scholars touch on the theme of freedom but mainly in relation to Catherine's involvement in the politics of her day; see, for example, Maria Francesca Carnea, *Libertà e politica in S. Caterina da Siena: privilegio e conquista per un pensiero volitivo e attuale* (Rome: Vivere In, 2011). For a translation of this work in English, see Maria Francesca Carnea, "Freedom and Politics in St. Catherine of Siena," trans. Marialuisa Buratti, OP, in *Catherine of Siena: Essays on Her Life and Thought*, ed. Thomas McDermott (Chicago: New Priory Press, 2015), 43–70.

never writes as a detached intellectual. Her work is explosive. All around her she can see people oppressed and without hope, men and women enslaved by lies and injustice, their lives maimed and broken by the crippling fetters of fear and discouragement. For Catherine, as a result, freedom became almost an obsession. In her short life, she herself was such a force of freedom—and a force *for* freedom—that she seemed, at times, more like an element than a human being. On one occasion, putting to herself the question, "What is my nature?" she replied at once, "It is fire!"[4]

❀

The present work has three distinct parts:

Part One, "Bondage into Freedom," explores the liberating character of Catherine's teaching on freedom. Almost no other saint or mystic in the tradition has been able, like Catherine, to find words to express the enormous dignity human beings possess because of the gift of freedom. Those who are disciples of Christ, she makes bold to say, are "free masters" of themselves. But Catherine is, of course, well aware of just how hard it is in practice to attain this level of freedom. What I find impressive to observe in the life and work of Catherine is how she is able to balance a bold, demanding vision of human perfection with the message of God's extraordinary compassion for the oppressed and struggling sinner. The final chapter of this first section is devoted to a comparison between Catherine's vision of freedom and that of the celebrated Renaissance philosopher Giovanni Pico della Mirandola. This chapter has a more academic character than the previous two chapters. Its purpose, however, is not primarily or exclusively academic. Few subjects since the time

---

4. Prayer 12, in *The Prayers of Catherine of Siena*, 2nd edition, trans. Suzanne Noffke (San Jose: Author's Choice, 2001), 117. (Hereafter, this work will be referred to simply as *Prayers*.)

of the Renaissance have been more discussed than freedom. It is of no small interest, therefore, to explore the extent to which St. Catherine's vision of freedom can still offer light and wisdom for some of the issues affecting society today.

Part Two, "Fire and Shadow: Catherine's Vision of the Self," is concerned first and last with the question of self-knowledge. Catherine's writing on this particular subject is remarkable. No aspect of her work and vision is more timely—and none more relevant to our age. But why, in a work that has as its principal focus the question of freedom, devote so much time and attention to a subject that might appear almost completely unrelated? To St. Catherine, as it happens, these two subjects—self-knowledge and freedom—are so intimately bound up together that should an individual fail to attain to at least a measure of authentic self-knowledge, that person will never be able to break free from the bondage of weakness, and never be able, as a result, to begin living life to the full. The first chapter in this section, "'Who Am I?' Catherine and Self-Knowledge," highlights Catherine's understanding of how weak and struggling men and women can come to discover the true "dignity and beauty" of their nature. This does not mean, of course, ignoring or covering over the sad, dark reality of sin and failure. Such things must be confronted and acknowledged, but only—Catherine insists—in the radiance of "the gentle mirror of God." The second chapter in this section sets out to explore the similarities and differences between St. Catherine's teaching on "the shadow" in self-knowledge and that of the modern depth psychologist Carl Gustav Jung. Jung was highly critical of what the medievals had to offer on the subject, but he would, I suspect, have been greatly surprised had he ever taken the opportunity to read Catherine of Siena.

Part Three focuses on some of the many ways in which the celebrated Dominican motto "Laudare, Benedicere, Praedicare" (To Praise, to Bless, to Preach) relates to the life and teaching of Catherine. While the first two sections are concerned principally with exploring St. Catherine's unique understanding of the path to freedom and self-knowledge as expressed in her writings, the third section gives particular attention to Catherine's *life*, to the way her pedagogy of freedom assumed vital and tangible form. This third and final section has three chapters:

- *"Laudare*: Freedom to Praise" gives attention to a number of the different ways in which Catherine prayed, noting some of the precise circumstances that occasioned her prayer. Catherine is a truly remarkable mystic: her life in general, and her life of prayer in particular, were graced with extraordinary favors. But what we find highlighted in her teaching is not the extraordinary way of mysticism but rather the ordinary Gospel path of prayer and contemplation. Everywhere evident in this chapter is the determining impact of the theological vision behind Catherine's prayer, her clear understanding of the marvel of the gift of human freedom, and her awareness of the dependence of that freedom on the saving "madness" of God's love for the world revealed in the Passion of Christ. Something of St. Catherine's unique spirit of freedom is evident also in her determination to participate fully in the celebration of the Divine Office of the Church, something that, at that time, was generally restricted to priests and nuns. Finally, the Gospel character of Catherine's focus on the neighbor is explored, specifically her insistence that without attention to the needs of the neighbor, there can be no authentic worship of God.

- "*Benedicere*: Freedom to Bless" takes up the question of St. Catherine's mystical encounter with God and of how that encounter, more than anything else in her life, opened her eyes to the wild tenderness of God's care for the most lost and most wretched of sinners. The company Catherine kept as a result—common criminals, public sinners, prostitutes, etc.—was a scandal to many of her contemporaries. They were inclined to judge and condemn, whereas Catherine's most immediate instinct, quickened by her own experience of divine mercy, was to call down a blessing not a curse. By freely welcoming all those most in need of mercy, by daring to look beyond the sin to the person, beyond the manifest crimes to the hidden wounds of hurt and self-disdain, Catherine brought to a great number of her contemporaries not only the balm of healing but also the sure promise of new life and freedom.

- "*Praedicare*: Freedom to Preach" focuses attention on how Catherine of Siena, a laywoman with no established role or title, was able to break free from many of the restrictions imposed on women at that time, and able also to play a vital role at the heart of both secular and ecclesiastical society. What emerges clearly is that the freedom Catherine enjoyed arose out of two things in particular: first and most obviously her friendship with God, the intimacy of which is often breathtaking; and, second, the extraordinary balance of her mystical intuition, in which elements of mercy and justice, humility and confidence, and love and fear are carefully and fearlessly ordered.

Many of the studies published on St. Catherine delight in speaking of her preaching on mercy but tend to ignore her teaching on the "four last things." My aim in this final section is to present as much as possible not only the enormous encouragement but also the enormous challenge of Catherine's preaching. Only then can one appreciate the unrelenting force of her desire to free people from their bondage, and begin also to grasp something of this young woman's profound understanding of the Good News of the Gospel, of which she is an inspired and gifted preacher.

Though Catherine's direct involvement in the social and political dramas of her time is of great significance, the lifeblood of her legacy is not to be found, at least not principally, in a detailed account of such involvement. However unique and important this involvement was, her true legacy is found in the passionate and lucid body of teaching that has come down to us in the *Dialogue* and in her letters and prayers.

CHRONOLOGY OF CATHERINE'S LIFE

1347   Catherine is born in Siena on March 25.

1348   The Bubonic Plague breaks out in Siena.

1353   Catherine has her first vision of Christ. She decides to dedicate her life to God.

c. 1364 Catherine joins the Mantellate, a group of laywomen in Siena. Instead, of joining in their ministry, she begins a three-year period of solitude and prayer, living in seclusion in a small room in her family house.

1368   Experience of mystical marriage with Christ. Catherine is called by Jesus to leave her solitude in order to serve the needy and the poor. A small group of disciples starts to form around her.

1370   Catherine undergoes a series of intense mystical experiences, culminating in what is sometimes referred to as a "mystical death."

1372   With the aim and hope of achieving peace between warring Italian states, Catherine writes her first political letters.

1374   Catherine is summoned to a General Chapter of the Dominican order "to render an account of herself and her conduct in the way of God." Raymond of Capua is assigned as her spiritual director. A fresh outbreak of the plague strikes Siena. Catherine tends the sick and the dying.

1375   Catherine journeys to Pisa. She preaches the crusade of Pope Gregory XI to retake the Holy Land, and works to maintain peace between the States of Italy and the papacy.

1376   On March 31, Florence is placed under papal interdict. At the request of the Florentines, Catherine goes to the pope at Avignon to intercede for them. She asks the pope to return to Rome. Gregory XI leaves Avignon for Rome on September 13.

1377   On January 17, Pope Gregory finally arrives in Rome. During the summer, Catherine travels to Val d'Orcia and engages in a mission of peace and reconciliation. In the autumn, after certain intense mystical experiences, she begins dictating *The Dialogue*.

1378   On March 27, Gregory XI dies. On April 8, Urban VI is elected. On September 20, the anti-pope Clement VII is elected, resulting in the Great Western Schism. In October, Catherine completes *The Dialogue*. On November 28, Catherine, along with about forty of her disciples, arrives in Rome to offer support to Urban. She stays in a house near the Minerva. In December, Raymond is sent by

Urban to France to address certain issues arising from the schism. Catherine never sees him again.

1379   In support of Pope Urban, Catherine sends letters and messages to almost every part of the Christian world. The majority of the prayers of Catherine that have been recorded belong to this period.

1380   Catherine's health deteriorates. Nevertheless, with enormous difficulty, she makes a mile-long journey every day to St. Peter's Basilica to pray for the Church. Although experiencing trials both spiritual and physical, she still finds the strength to dictate letters on behalf of the Church. Finally, on April 29, after several days and nights of mental and physical anguish, Catherine dies in the presence of her devoted community.

1461   On June 29, Catherine is canonized.

1939   On June 18, Pope Pius XII names Catherine co-patron of Italy along with St. Francis of Assisi.

1970   On October 4, Catherine is proclaimed a Doctor of the Church by Pope Paul VI.

I.
BONDAGE INTO FREEDOM

CHAPTER 1
"Freedom That Is a Woman"

"Why is that one gadding about so much? She's a woman. Why doesn't she stay in her cell, if it's God she wants to serve?"[1] According to the report of Blessed Raymond of Capua, the devoted friend and spiritual director of Catherine, these were the sorts of complaints that she had to endure for years—even within the confines of Siena itself. A great part of her life, Raymond tells us, was spent "in the give and take of social intercourse." She was gifted with "an outgoing affability" and "a charming graciousness in her dealings with others."[2] But some people—and "many pious people" among them—were unimpressed. A number of them, in fact, were outraged by the freedom of movement Catherine seemed to enjoy. Like St. Dominic before her, Catherine—in both the way she thought and the way she lived—was someone stupefyingly free. If, for example, she found that truth or justice were ever at stake, she did not hesitate to speak her mind to popes and politicians, hermits and cardinals, prostitutes, priests, and bounty hunters.

---

1. Raymond of Capua, *The Life of Catherine of Siena*, no. 365, trans. C. Kearns (Wilmington, DE: Glazier, 1980), 339. (Hereafter, this work will be referred to simply as *Life*.)

2. *Life*, no. 365, 339. Something of the great warmth of Catherine's character is indicated by a chance remark she made once concerning the small children having fun in her mother's kitchen: "If decency allowed it, I would never stop kissing them!" *Supplementum* (T. Caffarini's addition to Raymond of Capua's *Life*, trans. A. Tantucci, I, II, 12 [Lucca 1754], cited in Kenelm Foster, "Introduction," *I, Catherine: Selected Writings of Catherine of Siena*, trans. Kenelm Foster and Mary John Ronayne (London: Collins, 1980), 19. Hereafter, this work will be referred to simply as *I, Catherine*.)

❀

One of the saint's modern biographers, Johannes Jorgenson, remarks that when he began his research on Catherine, he found he was far more in sympathy with Francis of Assisi, the celebrated saint of nature, than with the young and exuberant visionary from Siena. But his continued engagement with Catherine's life and writings would challenge this initial impression. "Gradually," Jorgenson writes, "as I began to know her more intimately, the same thing befell me that befell so many others during her earthly life."[3] What happened, of course, was that by becoming more familiar with the writings of Catherine, and by learning more and more about her life and work, the saint of Siena began to capture and hold fast his attention. For all those drawn to the person and work of the Sienese saint, it's worth asking if a way can be found to describe not only the distinctive nature of her mission but also the compelling impact that she made on her immediate contemporaries and continues to make today.

Radical poverty, we know, was one of the primary elements of the spirituality of St. Francis. The joyous troubadour of Assisi was happy to declare to all that he had espoused himself to *la donna povertà*, Lady Poverty. This is language that Catherine of Siena would certainly have understood. But Catherine's most immediate concern is somewhat different from that of Francis. Her concern, above all else, is that people—encouraged by the truth of the Gospel—should be able to break free from their bondage, and should elect *freedom* as their partner or spouse, referring on

---

3. Johannes Jorgensen, *Saint Catherine of Siena*, trans. Ingeborg Lund (London: Longmans, Green and Co., 1946), v.

one occasion not to Lady Poverty but to Lady Freedom (literally, "freedom that is a woman": "la libertà, che è donna").[4]

Often in her work Catherine also underlines the importance of choosing truth as one's spouse or bride.[5] In *The Dialogue* we read that, although St. Dominic (like St. Francis) "had chosen Queen Poverty as his bride," his "more proper object" was "the salvation of souls by the light of learning"—the task, in other words, of setting people free from the darkness of error.[6] To choose truth, as Catherine understands it, is at the same time to choose freedom, and to stand up without fear to the threats and lies of evil and oppression. For free will, in consort with truth, Catherine believes, is effectively imperturbable: "Free woman that she is, neither the devil nor anyone else can force her to sin any more than she chooses to."[7]

1. Freedom: "So wonderful a gift!"

In St. Catherine's understanding, the two most important gifts bestowed on our humanity at creation are those of intelligence and free will. In this regard, she agrees with her great visionary forerunner, Dante Alighieri. In the *Divine Comedy*, Dante writes,

---

4. Letter to Pietro Marchese del Monti, T 148, *Le Lettere*, vol. 2, Tommasèo edition (Florence: Giunti, 1940), 295. (Hereafter, this work will be referred to simply as *Le Lettere*.) Suzanne Noffke translates the phrase "la libertà, che è donna" as "Lady Freedom" (Letter to Pietro del Monte Santa Maria, T 148, *The Letters of Catherine of Siena*, vol. 1 [Tempe, AZ: ACMRS, 2000], 151. [Hereafter, the Noffke edition of Catherine's letters will be referred to simply as *Letters*.])

5. See, for example, Letter to Raymond of Capua, T 100, *Letters*, vol. 3 (Tempe, AZ: ACMRS, 2007), 42.

6. See *Catherine of Siena: The Dialogue*, 158, trans. Suzanne Noffke (New York: Paulist, 1980), 337. (Hereafter, this work will be referred to simply as *Dialogue*.)

7. Letter to Don Cristofano, T 335, *Letters*, 2:585. In another place, Catherine describes the fortress of the soul when fully liberated from the devil's tyranny as "free and a woman" (*libera e donna*) (Letter to Frate Simone and Others, T 36, *Letters*, 2:128).

"The greatest gift God gave in creation . . . and the one he accounts the most precious of all was freedom of will. It was given to men and women endowed with intelligence, to them and to no one else."[8] Dante's statement is reflective, profound. Catherine's version, no less profound, is an uncontainable rush of thought and feeling, an outburst of praise. Thinking back on the gift of freedom bestowed upon us at creation, she exclaims: "O inestimable and sweetest fire of love, how clearly [with this gift] you show forth and make manifest the excellence of your creature!"[9] Once, while rapt in prayer—it was late February 1379—Catherine affirmed, with one tiny phrase, both the incomparable dignity of the Father and our own human dignity: "You alone," she declared, "are greater than we" (Solo tu se' maggiore di noi).[10]

Readers who come to Catherine's work for the first time might well expect to find in her writing a clear and comprehensive outline of the nature of the themes that engage her attention most urgently, such as human freedom. But the manner in which Catherine communicates her wisdom and knowledge is radically different from that of a speculative theologian. Her insights into the innermost source of human freedom, for example, are illumined and revelatory, though they are not expressed with the sharp precision and clarity we associate with someone like Aquinas.

Catherine gives particular attention to the question of freedom when describing the gates that guard "the city of the soul." There are three of them—"memory, understanding, and will"—and the one that she considers to be by far the strongest is the will.[11] The

8. Dante Alighieri, *Paradiso*, V, lines 19–24.
9. Letter to Sano di Maco, T 69, *Le Lettere*, vol. 1 (Florence: Giunti, 1940), 263.
10. Oratio VIII, *S. Caterina da Siena: Le Orazioni*, ed. G. Cavallini (Rome: Edizioni Cateriniane, 1978), 94.
11. Letter to Stefano Maconi, T 319, *Letters*, vol. 4, trans. Suzanne Noffke (Tempe, AZ: ACMRS, 2008), 3–4.

other two gates, understanding and memory, being in Catherine's judgement somehow more vulnerable, can on occasion fail to measure up to their task. She writes: "It sometimes happens that our understanding sees nothing but darkness," and "our memory is busy with empty and passing things."[12] The one "gate," therefore, "wholly under our control," the one that we possess "in total freedom," is our will.[13] "This gate," Catherine notes further, "has freedom of choice as its guard. . . . And if this gate remains unopened, that is, if we don't consent to what our memory and understanding and the other gates are sensing, our city is forever free."[14]

The disciple with whom Catherine is sharing these thoughts about human freedom is her close friend from Siena, Stefano Maconi. "So, let's acknowledge, son," she declares, "let's acknowledge so wonderful a gift, such boundlessly generous charity as we've received from divine Goodness. Since God has given us free possession of such a noble city, let's work hard to guard it well."[15] Catherine, writing two years earlier on the same theme to a cardinal in Avignon, made bold to declare: "God has made man free and powerful over himself" (Ha fatto l'uomo libero e potente sopra di sè).[16] This almost godlike power, this extraordinary grace, was bestowed on humanity at the moment of creation, when men and women were formed in the image and likeness of God.

After the subsequent loss of freedom, owing to the Fall, this power, this grace, was wonderfully restored by Christ: "The Lamb," Catherine declares, "gave himself up to the shameful death of the

---

12. Letter to Stefano Maconi, T 319, *Letters*, 4:4.
13. *Letters*, 4:4.
14. *Letters*, 4:4.
15. *Letters*, 4:4.
16. Letter to Pietro Cardinale Portuense, T 177, *Le Lettere*, vol. 3 (Florence: Giunti, 1940), 93.

most holy cross in order to restore our liberty and make us free.
. . . With unarmed hand he has conquered our enemies and has
given us back our freedom of choice."[17] We have, as a result, been
made "masters of ourselves"[18] and, at the same time, "free masters
of the world."[19] Here Catherine is daring to paint for us what is, in
effect, the ideal image of human freedom. She writes: "Those who
are masters of themselves have become masters of all the world.
For they neither fear nor care about anything except the things
of God, whom they love and serve."[20] Writing elsewhere on the
nature of God's goodness, Catherine declares: "He is so kind that
to serve him is more to reign than to be a servant. God makes all
his servants kings and queens, free lords and ladies, for he has
freed them from slavery to the devil and from blind servitude to
the perverse tyranny of the world."[21]

2. Church and State: Freedom in Chains

For Catherine there is, in the Christian life, no gift greater than
freedom. It means not only liberation from the power of sin
(and, with that, the ability to choose what is good and true and
to reject what is evil and false); it means also a new and open
access to intimate union with God. It is, in effect, among the
most distinguishing marks of the new life of grace. This fact,
and the manifest enthusiasm that Catherine shows for anything
connected with human dignity and freedom, goes some way to

---

17. Letter to Bernabò Visconti of Milan, T 28, *Letters*, 1:134.
18. Letter to Tommaso d'Alviano, T 259, *Letters*, vol. 2 (Tempe, AZ: ACMRS, 2001), 615.
19. Letter to Sano di Maco di Mazzacorno, T 62, *Letters*, 2:606.
20. Letter to Tommaso d'Alviano, T 259, *Letters*, 2:615.
21. Letter to Madonna Jacoma, widow of Messer Trincio de' Trinci, T 264, *Letters*, 2:481–82.

explain the stark character of her distress when she finds so many of her contemporaries willing to hand over their freedom to the power of the devil. "Everywhere I see people handing him the keys of free choice with perverse willingness: lay folk, religious, clerics are running pridefully to worldly enjoyment, prestige, and riches full of wretched filth!"[22]

In particular, Catherine could see that people occupying seats of power in her own city had sadly become slaves to their need for money and high position. Allowing themselves to be "tainted by human flattery," they failed again and again to bring to justice individuals of worldly influence known to have committed an offense. "To the poor, on the other hand, who haven't been guilty of one-thousandth of that offense, they mercilessly mete out harsh punishments."[23] Catherine, clearly appalled by the injustice she is forced to witness in her own city, can barely contain her anger: "The wretches," she declares, "appointed to govern the city (but who can't even govern themselves) often turn away to keep from seeing when poor men and women are being robbed; they give them not a bit of justice but turn away lest those deprived of justice should receive it."[24] Enslaved by human greed and lust for power, these men, the so-called "Lord Defenders of the People and Commune of Siena," had ended up oppressing and enslaving others.

---

22. Letter to Pope Gregory XI, T 270, *Letters*, 2:244. It is Catherine's conviction that once freedom is surrendered to the seduction of evil, we lose our human dignity: "We lose the light of reason and take on the existence of animals, who live irrationally. Oh human blindness! To what greater misery can we sink than to be brute beasts? If someone were to say to us, 'You are a beast!' we couldn't bear it. In fact, we would try to take revenge on the person who said it. And yet our weakness is so great that we turn ourselves into beasts" (Letter to Giovanna, Queen of Naples, T 362, *Letters*, 4:223).

23. Letter to the Lord Defenders of the People and Commune of Siena, T 367, *Letters*, 4:321.

24. *Letters*, 4:321.

For Catherine what was even more terrible to contemplate was the phenomenon of rank corruption within the Church, corruption in the lives of priests, religious, and cardinals. "As you know," she writes, "God demands integrity and purity of such men. But—alas![25]—Venerable father, God is finding just the opposite: not only are they themselves corrupt and putrid, but they corrupt all who come near them!"[26] Catherine, at this point, is writing to a parish priest at Asciano. Her letter, from start to finish, is a veritable lament. "We blindly sell ourselves to the devil," she declares, adding—as if without taking a breath—"I beg you for love of Christ crucified: let's get out of such slavery!"[27] And again: "It's up to us to use the freedom we have been given to choose life or death."[28]

3. The Recovery of Freedom

Over and over again this same urgent appeal, now in one form, now in another, is made by Catherine to her contemporaries. Her one overwhelming concern, as the extracts below from her letters indicate, is that all should seize the opportunity afforded by Christ to live free from the oppression of sin and weakness:

> Christ frees us from weakness and strengthens the heart of the troubled who with genuine humility and confidence ask for his help.[29]

> Oh how sweet is this servitude that frees us from the servitude of sin![30]

---

25. Here and elsewhere in the present work I have inserted the word "alas" for the Italian word "oimé," which Noffke has chosen to leave untranslated.

26. Letter to Biringhieri degli Arzocchi, parish priest of Asciano, T 24, *Letters*, 2:156.

27. *Letters*, 2:158.

28. *Letters*, 2:157.

29. Letter to Madonna Jacoma, T 264, *Letters*, 2:479.

30. Letter to Pietro del Monte Santa Maria, T 180, *Letters*, 1:192.

Free yourselves from the bond of pride and bind yourselves to the humble Lamb.[31]

We must, then, very conscientiously free our heart and affection from this tyrant, the world, and set it on God, completely free and sincere, letting nothing come between ourselves and him. We must not be two-faced or love falsely, since he is our dear God, and he keeps his eyes on us, seeing our hidden and inmost heart.[32]

I long, with boundless love, for God in his infinite mercy to free you from all halfheartedness and sentimentality and make you a new man.[33]

We will do, then, what the Canaanite woman did. As we see Christ passing through our soul we will turn to him in true holy desire, with sincere contrition and hatred for sin, and we will say: "Lord, free my daughter—I mean my soul!"[34]

The actual forms of slavery from which Catherine desires to liberate her contemporaries include such things as slavery to sin, to oppression, to lies and fear, and to the threat of death. But even more than her concern to liberate people *from* various kinds of oppression, Catherine's focus, in her writings and in her prayers, is on the positive use and purpose of freedom—what freedom is *for*. This means in practice the freedom to choose to live a life of virtue in service of the Gospel; the freedom to work not for one's own immediate aims but for justice and truth; the freedom, in short, to devote oneself wholeheartedly to the love of God and neighbor.

---

31. Letter to Buonaccorso di Lapo, T 234, *Letters*, 2:241.
32. Letter to Tora Gambacorta, T 194, *Letters*, 4:256.
33. Letter to Pope Gregory XI, T 255, *Letters*, 2:192.
34. Letter to Sano di Maco di Mazzacorno, T 69, Letters, 1:65.

And it means also freedom to open oneself up in contemplation to the love of God in Christ, turning one's gaze to God with what Catherine calls the eye of faith and understanding. She writes: "If our free will chooses to open this eye and focus it on Christ crucified and his pure, tender, straightforward love for us, we will on seeing his straightforwardness receive him straightforwardly into our affection and will."[35] What's more, "With the love we have drawn from the gentle loving Word, we will love our neighbors, love them purely, faithfully seeking their salvation and helping them to the best of our ability with whatever God has given us to administer."[36] In the end, in Catherine's understanding, it is only the pure, tender, straightforward love of God revealed in Christ Jesus that can rescue men and women from the slavery of pride and selfishness, and help liberate them to use the freedom they have been given for great and noble aims.

---

35. Letter to Misser Niccolò da Uzzano, T 199, *Letters*, 3:101.
36. *Letters*, 3:101.

CHAPTER 2
Fear into Freedom:
The Liberating Message of Catherine

Freedom to think and freedom to act: these are the two forms of freedom that, in Catherine's opinion, mark our dignity as human beings. Needless to say, then, any loss of that dignity is for Catherine an unspeakable tragedy. Nothing distresses her more than the sight of free men and women reduced by the pressure of their own weakness, or by the pressure of the society in which they live, to a debilitating moral servitude. Almost every page of her writing is, as a result, an impassioned manifesto of freedom. Wherever she finds herself, whatever she is doing or saying or thinking, her attention is focused—with great intensity—on the wretched state of her contemporaries.

Often, we are inclined to think of mystics as people whose contemplation focuses entirely on God and the nature of God. But, to a degree almost unique among the Christian saints and mystics, Catherine was contemplative also of human nature, of both its misery and its grandeur. In particular, she understood an aspect of our human condition and of our human psychology that, over the last two hundred years, has begun to receive increasing attention from both psychologists and philosophers—namely, the psychology of fear.

1. Fear as an Enemy

For the majority of spiritual authors, it has always been enough simply to address what they perceived as the three most obvious enemies of freedom: the world, the flesh, and the devil. But Catherine in a sense goes further and deeper. With a quite remarkable grace of insight, she uncovers, at the root of human weakness and human distress, the face of fear. And she names for us—now in one letter, now in another—some of the many different forms that fear assumes, noting for example how afraid we can become of other people, of what they think of us and of how they judge us; afraid of death and suffering, or of God's judgment; or afraid even of ourselves, of our own weakness and our spiritual and moral failure. "Oh how dangerous such fear is!" she writes. "It cuts off the arms of holy desire. It binds us and keeps us from knowing the truth."[1]

That Catherine regards fear as one of the most deadly enemies of freedom is clearly indicated by the fact that she refers to it almost always as "slavish fear" (*un timore servile*)—something, in other words, that takes our liberty away from us, reducing us to abject slaves. The phrase *timore servile* occurs in a few letters sent by Catherine to Pope Gregory XI: "I long," she wrote, "to see you a courageous man, free of slavish fear."[2] And, again, some months later: "I have asked and will continue to ask the good gentle Jesus to free you from all slavish fear, leaving you only holy fear."[3] In both Catherine's letters and in *The Dialogue*, we find another short phrase closely connected to *timore servile*—namely, "the wind of fear."[4] When, according to Catherine, this wind gathers strength and begins to attack us from within, the very life of our soul is at risk, for instead of flourishing and becoming healthy "trees of love," we become "trees of death."[5] So powerful in its impact is

---

1. Letter to Pierre d'Estaing, T 11, *Letters*, 2:522.
2. Letter to Pope Gregory XI, T 229, *Letters*, 2:190.
3. *Letters*, 2:212. For Catherine's understanding of "holy fear," see Letter T 361, *Letters*, 4:67.
4. *Dialogue*, no. 94, 175.
5. *Dialogue*, no. 94, 175.

"the wind of slavish fear"[6] that we begin to be afraid even of our own shadow, our lives continually battered and shaken by "the contrary winds of devilish or creaturely vexations that would like to get in the way of our salvation."[7]

2. The Power of Free Will

What is Catherine's response to the threat posed by these "contrary winds"? First, to anyone prepared to listen, she declares that, as human beings, we in fact already possess an enormous strength—a "treasure" Catherine calls it—something so powerful that none of the enemies of freedom can hold out against it.[8] And that power is, of course, free will itself. In a letter to a friend, she asks: "What is this thing that is ours, given us by God, that neither the devil nor anyone else can take from us?" And she replies: "It is our will."[9] And again, in a letter to the Lord of Sanseverino, she writes: "This gentle God has given us the strength of our will, which is the soul's fortress, and neither the devil nor anyone else can take it away from us. Certainly, then, we can be secure and fearless."[10]

Catherine is obviously determined to drive home the point that, although we may feel under enormous pressure at times, we have in fact sufficient strength to match that pressure. She writes: "No one can force us to commit the slightest sin, because God has put *yes* and *no* into the strongest thing there is, into our will."[11] In a similar vein, writing to a group of young monks—all of them natives of Siena—Catherine goes so far as to describe free will as

---

6. *Dialogue*, no. 94, 175.
7. Letter to Countess Bandeçça Salimbeni, T 113, *Letters*, 2:681.
8. Letter to Sano di Maco, T 69, *Letters*, 1:65.
9. Letter to Monna Bartolomea, T 165, *Letters*, 2:40.
10. Letter to Bartolomeo Smeducci, G I, *Letters*, 1:185.
11. Letter to Bernabò Visconti, T 28, *Letters*, 1:133.

a "pick-axe." And she declares that no matter what difficulty may be confronting the monks, the innate strength of their willpower will assure them of final victory. She writes: "Your will is master of this wall, and with the pick-axe of free choice can maintain or demolish it as it chooses."[12]

The young visionary also adopts this tough, virile approach elsewhere, in particular when she is writing to people whom she knows possess great natural strength and energy, such as the famous tyrant, Bernabò Visconti of Milan.[13] In her letter to Bernabò, Catherine encourages him to confront directly those enemies of the spirit who would rob him of his own inner freedom: "Strike those enemies down," she says, "with the hand of free choice. Do not hesitate, for this hand is strong, this sword powerful . . . and no one can wrest it from you."[14] Writing to her friend Stefano Maconi, Catherine adopts a tone no less sharp and direct: "Be a manly man who advances courageously to the battlefield. Keep before your mind's eye the blood shed with such blazing love, so that you may be inspired for battle, entirely free."[15]

That was in December 1378. A few weeks later, in a further letter to Stefano, Catherine speaks of the need to run "free and unbound in the teaching of Christ crucified."[16] It's clear that Catherine is not prepared to entertain for a moment the idea that moral evil is unavoidable. She seizes every opportunity, in fact, to convince us that we are much stronger than we realize. "If we

---

12. Letter to Frate Simone di Giovanni and others, T 36, *Letters*, 2:128. In the same letter (127) Catherine writes: "I beg you, my dear sons in Christ gentle Jesus: never be afraid." And again (128): "Never ever be afraid of anything—neither the apprehension about not being able to persevere, nor the prospect that bearing up under obedience and the rule may be painful, nor anything that might happen."

13. Bernabò Visconti (1323–1385) was a tyrant opposed to the papacy. For thirty years he dominated Italian politics.

14. Letter to Bernabò Visconti, T 28, *Letters*, 1:134.

15. Letter to Stefano Maconi, T 205, *Letters*, 4:40.

16. Letter to Stefano Maconi, T 222, *Letters*, 4:77.

were not free we would have an excuse for sin. But we can have no excuse because there is nothing, neither the world nor the devil nor our weak flesh, that can force us to any sin at all against our will."[17]

3. Listening to the Voices of the Weak

Catherine's enormous confidence in the strength of free will, and her repeated assertion that determination of will alone can triumph over all the enemies of freedom, pays an enormous compliment to the potential or actual strength of human beings. But Catherine is not naïve. She knows very well just how weak and frail human nature can be, and how all too easily "we lose our mastery and become the servants and slaves of sin."[18] Had she simply declared that "there is no excuse for sin" and left it at that, her teaching would have offered little or no hope to the struggling sinner. But Catherine never forgets the enormous difference that the death of Christ has made for the weakest among us. It's true, we have no excuse for sin; and yet, Catherine notes, Christ made excuses for us as he was dying on the cross: "For when the Jews shouted 'Crucify!' he cried out, 'Father, forgive them, for they don't know what they are doing.' Oh limitless goodness of God! Not only does he forgive them but he makes excuses for them before the Father! He is a gentle lamb and never a cry or complaint is heard from him."[19]

---

17. Letter to Countess Bandeçça Salimbeni, T 113, *Letters*, 2:677. In the *Dialogue* the Father says to Catherine: "The soul is free, liberated from sin in my Son's blood, and she cannot be dominated unless she consents to it with her will, which is bound up with free choice. Free choice is one with the will and agrees with it. It is set between sensuality and reason and can turn to whichever one it will" (*Dialogue*, no. 52, 105).

18. Letter to Sano di Maco, T 69, *Letters*, 1:66.

19. Letter to Giovanni Perotti, T 156, *Letters*, 1:300–301.

God, out of compassion for fallen humanity—Catherine loves to repeat—"became a servant to make us free" and to rescue us from the death of sin. Nevertheless, "every day," she confesses, "we fall into this same eternal death by overstepping God's gentle will."[20] This revealing admission, one often repeated by Catherine, is a statement that, for the sake of balance, needs to be placed alongside her earlier and truly bold declaration that we are "masters of ourselves." Catherine is willing to affirm again and again the innate strength and power of the human will, but she is also prepared to acknowledge, with no less frequency, how hard it is in practice to free ourselves from the bondage of sin and weakness. Although Catherine believes that the fundamental damage caused by original sin has been overcome by the saving power of Christ's blood, this does not mean that it is now easy to avoid falling into sin. On the contrary, in a letter to Stefano Maconi, she remarks: "In Christ's blood we are made strong, even though weakness persists in our sensuality."[21]

In this context, what most distinguishes Catherine as a spiritual guide is her willingness to listen to the voices of those people around her who despair of ever being able to break free from their bondage. It comes as no surprise, therefore, to find space in her letters for such voices to be heard. For example, in one letter sent to her in early January 1376, we come upon the following declaration: "I can't pursue that sort of perfection; I feel that I am frail and weak and imperfect. I am worn down by the devil's wiles, by the weakness of my flesh, by the world's allurements and deceit."[22] Confronted with such clear manifestations of distress,

---

20. Letter to Pietro del Monte, T 180, *Letters*, 1:192.
21. Letter to Stefano Maconi, T 195, *Letters*, 4:69.
22. Letter to Bishop Angelo Ricasoli, T 88, *Letters*, 1:228. See also T 13, *Letters*, 4:16.

Catherine knows that it is not enough to offer a discourse on the outstanding gift of freedom and deliver sharp and robust commands. Although not averse, on occasion, to using the tough language employed by someone like Dante Alighieri when addressing sinners, Kenelm Foster reminds us that Catherine "had this advantage over the great poet": "that from girlhood she had spent herself on behalf of sinners and outcasts, had struggled with the demon of despair in the hearts of lepers and condemned criminals."[23]

Drawing on many years of experience, Catherine knew that an individual can become so totally caught up in the coils of sin that he or she begins to suffer a virtual moral paralysis. Should this happen, the sinner, in Catherine's understanding, is not just wicked or worldly. The sinner is *afraid*. He has become "weak" and "fearful" and "slavishly timid," and is afraid even of his "own shadow."[24] People who find themselves thus reduced—their lives utterly and completely dominated by sin—become, the Father explains to Catherine, "unbearable to themselves."[25] But in this extremity, there still remains one way in which their freedom can be expressed, and that is by turning to God and asking for help. "But that," the Father makes clear, "is the limit of what they can do for themselves."[26]

Writing on one occasion to a friend who had been suffering great discouragement—his name was Sano di Maco—Catherine pleads that he not lose heart in his struggle with evil, but instead

---

23. Foster, "Introduction," *I, Catherine*, 18–19. On this same point Cornelio Fabro remarks: "The saint [Catherine of Siena] knows very well that she is speaking with men and not with angels and the seraphim. She knows the heartaches of life and the troubles of conscience where freedom is sometimes confronted by obstacles and difficulties which appear to make the realization of freedom impossible" ("Mutuo accrescimento di libertà e grazia secondo S. Caterina," 61. See also Carnea, *Libertà e politica in S. Caterina da Siena*, 102).

24. Letter to Bishop Angelo Ricasoli, T 88, Letters, 1:228.

25. *Dialogue*, no. 31, 73.

26. *Dialogue*, no. 31, 73.

remain "a true and courageous knight."[27] Her letter reveals two things: an absolute confidence, first of all, in the power of God to rescue this "dearest, very loved brother and son"[28] from all the attacks of the enemy; and second, her awareness of just how difficult in practice the struggle can be.

> If, dearest son, you say to me, "I am weak in the face of so many enemies," I answer you that of ourselves we are all so weak and frail that we fall at the slightest obstacle. But divine providence is at work within our soul, strengthening us and relieving us of all weakness. So be trustful, firmly believing that God always provides for souls who trust in him. Then the devil is powerless, because the power of the most gracious holy cross deprives him of all his power over us. But that same cross, by God's boundless goodness, makes us wholly strong, freed from all weakness and instability.[29]

In the same year in which Catherine wrote this letter to Sano di Maco, she wrote to a senator of Siena called Pietro del Monte, expressing her desire that he also remain strong—"a courageous and fearless knight"—in the struggle against evil.[30] An individual such as him, she remarks, "who knows he is well armed, ought not to be afraid," for "God has equipped us with armor so strong it cannot be pierced by the devil or by anyone else."[31] That armor, she goes on to explain, is the unique protection afforded us by the gift of free will—"la libertà, che è donna" (Lady Freedom).[32] She writes: "Now God wants us to make use of the armor he has given

---

27. Letter to Sano di Maco, T 142, *Letters*, 1:76.

28. A phrase Catherine uses in another letter to describe Sano (T 147, *Letters*, 1:74).

29. Letter to Sano di Maco, T 142, *Letters*, 1:76.

30. Letter to Pietro del Monte, T 148, *Letters*, 1:150.

31. *Letters*, 1:150–151.

32. Letter to Pietro del Monte, T 148, *Letters*, 1:151.

us; he wants us to use it to deflect the blows our enemies inflict on us. We have three specific enemies: the world, the flesh, and the devil. But let's not be afraid, because divine providence has fitted us so well that we have no reason for fear."[33]

4. Freedom: The Gift and the Giver

Catherine, by placing the gift of free will front and center, would seem to have offered a full and complete answer to the question regarding the help we need in order to be protected from the assaults of our enemies. But in Catherine's letter to Pietro, she offers another important perspective on this "help" that relates directly to the task of prayer and contemplation. For, as well as relying on the actual *gift* of freedom, we are reminded by Catherine never to forget the *Giver*, for only by keeping our attention fixed on this "best helper" will we be able to achieve final freedom and lasting protection. "Our helper," she writes, "is God, and he is such that no one can withstand him. As long as we continue to look to this strong loving helper, we cannot be weakened by the thought of our own frailty."[34]

That contemplative focus on divine love is, for Catherine, absolutely crucial if we are to find the courage and strength to overcome our bondage to weakness and sin. Should an individual, therefore, be brought to the point of despair by the bondage of weakness, that man or that woman should go to God like a child going to its mother, bringing all its fear and all its weakness into the presence of love. Catherine explains that love—the "wondrous charity" of God—is the "gentlest of mothers."[35] It is the "remedy

---

33. *Letters*, 1:151.
34. *Letters*, 1:151.
35. Letter to Bishop Angelo Ricasoli, T 88, *Letters*, 1:229.

for all our weakness."[36] Accordingly, it is to the great charity of God that the sinner should run, just the way a child, "if sensible and wise, will fly to its mother, and in her womb become secure, and lose all fear."[37] Catherine is well aware that "the enemies besieging us are many,"[38] but confident that in God we have a true refuge, and that "charity," or the love of God, "does away with weakness and makes us strong."[39] She concludes: "Stay near your gentle mother, charity, who will free you from all servile fear and all coldness of heart, and give you strength, and breadth, and freedom of heart."[40]

❄

Apart from the question of human weakness, there is the related question of human suffering. What kind of advice can the saint offer to the individual who has been caught in a storm of cruel circumstances and has been deeply wounded as a result? How can that individual be content to accept the will of God when the pain he is enduring brings not pious thoughts but anger and rebellion? Catherine's first instinct when she encounters anyone reeling with great pain is first of all to be attentive, and then, without making rash judgements of any kind, to offer whatever practical help she can.[41] By all accounts she was endowed with a strong, impetuous temperament. So Catherine would have understood very well the temptation to impatient anger and revolt. What advice, then, does she give in such a circumstance?

---

36. *Letters*, 1:229.
37. Letter to Angelo Ricasoli, T 88, *Le Lettere*, 2:77.
38. *Le Lettere*, 2:80.
39. *Le Lettere*, 2:80.
40. *Le Lettere*, 2:79–80.
41. Eloquent, in this context, is the story of the devoted attention that Catherine gave to a very sick woman in Siena called Tecca. Leprosy had broken out all over this poor woman's body. As a result, she was consumed with bitterness and rage, mocking all the efforts that Catherine made to help her. But this did not prevent the saint from carrying out her task. According to Blessed Raymond, she "bowed low in body and in spirit before this abject sufferer" (*Life*, nos. 143–146, 138–141).

As it happens, the counsel Catherine offers is strikingly similar to the advice she gives when speaking about human weakness. In a letter to Nella Buonconti, who was undergoing certain trials, Catherine begins by acknowledging first of all how bewildering, and at times wounding, the shocks and hurts we all experience on life's journey can be: "We cannot cross this sea without troubles assaulting us no matter where we turn. This sea batters us with its waves, and the devil with all his temptations. And more: what the devil can't do himself he does by using other people."[42]

Catherine then goes on to explain how the Evil One can put into people's heads certain negative thoughts about the lives of their neighbors that have no basis in reality. But, trusting in the mystery of divine providence, Catherine makes bold to declare that God permits these waves to assault us. One unfortunate but all too human response in such a circumstance is to "lift up our head against our Creator, and be unwilling to suffer."[43] But the saint actively discourages a response of this kind, remarking: "I have never seen a single burden relieved by impatience." She adds: "If you want to be relieved of your burdens and infirmities, keep your eyes on the slain, consumed Lamb, so that the fire of his charity may warm your heart and soul to love for patience and consume all the cold and damp of selfish sensual love and passion and self-pity."[44]

The message is as bold as it is clear, suggesting to those held captive by either great hurt, great fear, or great anger that there is

---

42. Letter to Nella Buonconti, T 151, *Letters*, 2:457.
43. *Letters*, 2:459.
44. *Letters*, 2:459. That experience of "fire," Catherine explains in another place, brings about a new freedom. For by devoting our whole attention to the "blazing love" revealed in "the blood of the spotless Lamb," and by drinking in that love, absorbing that knowledge "little by little," she declares, "we find we've become drunk—for a drunkard loses all sense of self and feels nothing but the sense of the wine, with every feeling immersed in the wine. So it is with us when we have become drunk on the blood of Christ. Freed from sensual love and freed from sensual fear (since there is no fear of pain where there is no sensual love), we even find joy in suffering" (Letter to Frate Tommaso dalla Fonte, T 25, *Letters*, 3:57–58.

a way to attain a level of serene freedom, no matter how many or how frightening the troubles assaulting them. It is a message that has its origin in the great spiritual tradition, a teaching that earlier in the letter prompted Catherine to compose the following brief hymn to the virtue of patience:

> O true, oh lovely patience! You are the virtue that is never overcome. No, it is you who triumph. You give us hope for glory. You dissolve hatred and animosity in the heart and liberate us from contempt for our neighbors. You free our souls from pain. You make the heavy weight of hardships light, and because of you bitter things become sweet.[45]

Mary Ann Fatula, reflecting on the enlightening paradoxical wisdom in St. Catherine's teaching on suffering, remarks:

> Catherine endured tragedy herself and suffered with friends as they grieved bitter losses. But her own experience taught her that even the most cruel sufferings hide within them the tenderness of God's will and the treasure of his infinite love. As she reflected on the meaning of our pain in the light of Jesus' own death, she found that under the "bitter rind" a sweet fruit lies hidden. God can draw forth even from the ashes of our broken lives the most radiant joy and new life. If we pray for the grace not to resist God's "sweet will," the Lord's own love can heal our wounds and free our hearts for even deeper growth.[46]

The focus of Catherine's attention in her "hymn" to the virtue of patience is on freedom: freedom from pain, freedom from bitterness, and freedom from hatred. Those people who possess this great virtue, she believes, learn to put their trust in the

45. Letter to Frate Tommaso dalla Fonte, T 25, *Letters*, 3:56–57. For a no less eloquent tribute to the virtue of patience, see *Dialogue*, no. 77, 143–144.
46. Mary Ann Fatula, *Catherine of Siena's Way* (London: Darton, Longman and Todd, 1987), 55–56.

power of God to save rather than trusting merely in their own determined efforts. As a result, over time, they begin to experience true liberation and become almost fearless:

> They act like true knights who never consider any rising storm so great that they are daunted by it. They have no fear because it is not in themselves that they trust. No, all their faith and trust is in God, whom they love, because they see that he is strong, and that he is willing and able to help them. So, with Saint Paul they say very humbly, "I can do all things in Christ crucified, who is in me and who strengthens me."[47]

5. "No more fear!"

Of all the letters that touch on the theme of fear and freedom, perhaps the most impressive is a letter that Catherine sent to a married woman named Costanza Soderini. Catherine takes the trouble, first of all, to list a number of the fears that usually prevent us from being free. She writes:

> Sometimes people suffer a great deal from fear of death and because of their self-indulgence. The first is a delusion the devil puts in their minds. He says, "You see that you are going to die, and that you haven't done a bit of good! So do you know where you're going? Your deeds have earned only hell!" On the other hand, he makes them feel sorry for themselves by saying, "Just think! Your body is so pampered now with worldly pleasures, but soon you will die."[48]

The devil, Catherine explains, exploits the deepest human fears in order to lead people into "discouragement and despair":

---

47. Letter to Cardinal Iacopo Orsini, T 101, *Letters*, 2:70.
48. Letter to Costanza Soderini, T 314, *Letters*, 2:486.

"He wants them to see only their short-comings and sins, and to hide the divine mercy from them."[49] But how exactly are we supposed to respond in this type of situation? Catherine's answer shows two things: first, her sharp grasp of human psychology, and second, her profound understanding of the nature of God's mercy. She writes:

> We have to counter the devil's great malice by responding to these interior suggestions of his. Turning our gaze to our Creator, we should say, "I acknowledge that I am mortal, but this is a tremendous grace for me, since death will bring me to my goal, to God who is my life. I acknowledge, too, that my life and deeds deserve only hell. But I have faith and trust in my Creator, in the blood of the Lamb who was slain and consumed, that he will pardon my sins and grant me grace. I will try in this present time to amend my life. But if death should overtake me before I have amended my life—that is, before I have yet done penance for my sins—I still say that I trust *in Domine nostro Jesu Christo*, because I see that there is no comparison between my sins and divine mercy. Even if all the sins that could possibly be committed were gathered together in one person, it would be like a drop of vinegar in the sea."[50]

The message is clear: "No more fear!" Catherine continues:

> Live this bit of time in joy, with a desire for virtue. Bear patiently whatever physical or spiritual suffering God sends you, whether in the form of illness or in any other form. Don't let me see you evading suffering. For every pain you suffer is given you by God for your good, because he wants to reward you when you come in from the stormy sea of this darksome life and arrive at the place

---

49. Letter to Costanza Soderini, T 314, *Letters*, 2:486.
50. *Letters*, 2:486.

of rest, your true city, Jerusalem, vision of peace. There all our willingness to suffer, every good deed we have done in this life, is rewarded."[51]

Catherine assures Costanza that as soon as she begins "to pursue true solid virtue . . . drawing near to God," she will experience "utter joy and happiness and confidence," and "will lose all slavish fear."[52] Catherine then goes on to make a simple but impressive statement concerning God's mercy. Reminding Costanza of the saving death of Christ on the cross, Catherine writes: "There is such immense mercy in this that no human heart or language can possibly describe or even imagine it. Mercy, therefore, relieves us of fear and pain."[53]

❊

Catherine's first instinct, when she finds herself confronted by the anguish of people struggling to overcome sin and weakness, is to draw attention to the gift of free will, to the capacity all of us have to say no to wrongdoing of any kind. Conscious, however, of just how difficult it can be in practice to activate the will in this regard, Catherine also highlights the need we have as human beings to experience in faith something of the shock of the tenderness of God's love. Without that knowledge, that blessing, we will begin to lose heart, and will almost inevitably "fall at the slightest obstacle."[54] Although decidedly bold in many of her declarations regarding human freedom—and more than happy, therefore, to hold up before us the stout image of the sword and the axe of free choice—Catherine, being aware at the same time of just how

---

51. Letter to Costanza Soderini, T 314, *Letters*, 2:486–487.
52. *Letters*, 2:485.
53. *Letters*, 2:485–486.
54. Letter to Sano di Maco, T 142, *Letters*, 1:76.

great our need is as followers of the Gospel for living knowledge of God's love, paints for us also an image of a very different kind: that of a child running to its mother for help.

This wise and balanced teaching on freedom—the different ways in which Catherine is able to encourage the weak while never ignoring the reality of the gift of free will—is not only eminently practical and encouraging; it is also, by any standard, truly inspired.

CHAPTER 3
A Tale of Two Freedoms:
Catherine and Giovanni Pico
della Mirandola

A radical commitment to the ideal of human freedom is something almost never linked with the early or late Middle Ages—at least not in the popular mind. As a result, the strong advocacy of freedom by Catherine of Siena, a young medieval woman, will come as something of a surprise to many. Not only in her letters and in the *Dialogue* but even in a number of her most private and intimate prayers, Catherine's unerring focus on the question of freedom appears almost as a signature.

On one occasion, while Catherine was in Rome on the Feast of the Annunciation, she found herself reflecting in prayer on the words that, according to the Gospel, Mary had said to the angel—humble words of enormous consequence. The prayer of Catherine on this occasion is eloquent, first word to last—not only in expressing the singular freedom that Mary clearly enjoyed but also the gift of freedom that all human beings share.

> In you, O Mary, our human strength and freedom are today revealed, for . . . the angel was sent to you to announce to you the mystery of the divine counsel and to seek to know your will. And God's Son did not come down into your womb until you had given your will's consent. He waited at the door of your will for you to open to him; for he wanted to come into you, but he would never have entered unless you had opened to him, saying: "Here I am, God's servant; let it be done to me as you have said." The strength

and freedom of the will are clearly revealed, then. For no good nor any evil can be done without that will. . . . The eternal Godhead, oh Mary, was knocking at your door, but unless you had opened that door of your will God would not have taken flesh in you.[1]

On another occasion, when Catherine was caught up in ecstasy in prayer, this time at Avignon, the few friends and disciples who were present with her overheard Catherine speak briefly on the subject of free will. The creation of human beings was the main focus of her attention—the high mystery, that is, of our being made in the image of the Holy Trinity. Catherine begins her prayer: "Godhead! Godhead! Ineffable Godhead! O supreme Goodness who for love alone made us in your image and likeness."[2] Later she is heard to exclaim: "In whatever direction I turn I find unutterable love. . . . It is you alone, God and human, who loved me without my having loved you, for I did not exist and you made me."[3] Catherine knows it was for love, and for no other reason, that she was created by God, and then by grace recreated anew. Moved by this thought, she exclaims: "You have drawn me to yourself in unutterable love, and you draw all of us to yourself not because you must but freely."[4] For Catherine, the gift of freedom is nothing less than a sharing in God's own freedom. Our human "will," she tells us, by which in this context she means the gift of freedom in action, "reaches up like a hand . . . to take whatever our understanding knows of God's unutterable goodness."[5]

That image of the lifted hand—Catherine calls it "this strong hand of love"[6]—brings to mind Michelangelo's powerful fresco

---

1. Prayer 18, *Prayers*, 192–193.
2. Prayer 1, *Prayers*, 4.
3. *Prayers*, 6.
4. *Prayers*, 8.
5. *Prayers*, 4.
6. *Prayers*, 4.

of the creation of Adam in the Sistine Chapel: the hand of the first man on earth reaching out in serene, astonished wonder to the hand of his Creator. "Our will," Catherine writes, "wanting to love something, moves our understanding to see. And when our understanding senses that the will . . . wants to love, it centers its attention on the indescribable love of the eternal Father, who has given us the Word his Son. . . . And so, our will reaches out with indescribable love for what our understanding has seen."[7]

1. "I am making you free"

Approximately one hundred years after the death of Catherine, one of the most important philosophers of the Renaissance, Giovanni Pico della Mirandola, became fascinated by the theme of freedom. In his treatise *Oratio: De hominis dignitate (Oration on the Dignity of Man)*, he declared that the human being was "a great miracle," and that nothing exists on earth that is more free or more magnificent.[8] This particular idea Pico traced back to an imagined conversation between God the Creator and Adam the first man. He wrote:

> God decided to create man in a form that is indefinite. He placed him at the center of the universe, and said to him: "We have not given you any particular place to dwell in, or particular appearance, or any function that is uniquely yours, O Adam, so that according to your own judgment and desire, you can have and possess for yourself any dwelling place, any appearance, any

---

7. Letter to Certain Florentine Youths, T 95, *Letters*, 2:568–569. For a helpful reflection on the relationship between will and intellect in the teaching of St. Catherine, see Fabro, "Mutuo accrescimento di libertà e grazia secondo S. Caterina," 62–64.

8. Giovanni Pico della Mirandola, *Oratio: Discorso sulla dignità dell'uomo* [text in Latin and Italian], ed. G. Tognon (Brescia: La Scuola, 1987), 2–3.

function you choose. . . . No barriers will stand in your way. You will determine your own nature according to your own free will. . . . I have placed you in the middle of the world so that you will be able from there to see with ease all that is in the world around you. We have made you neither celestial nor terrestrial, neither mortal nor immortal, so that, as the free and sovereign sculptor of your own being, you can fashion yourself into whatever image you choose."[9]

The passage is justly famous. It is not only one of the finest texts on human freedom ever composed, it is also a key text for understanding Renaissance humanism. But why, in a study devoted to Catherine's understanding of freedom, give attention to this particular extract from Pico's *Oratio*? Well, the main reason for citing it here is because Catherine, in one of her own writings, places on the lips of God the Creator a comparable statement concerning human freedom.

The passage in question occurs in a letter she wrote to Sano di Maco, one of her disciples in Siena.[10] In this letter, Catherine's immediate focus is a passage from Matthew 15 that records the meeting between Jesus and a Canaanite woman whose daughter was possessed by an evil spirit. The mother came to Jesus in great distress asking that her daughter be released from this terrible bondage. In response, Jesus replied: "Let your daughter . . . be healed *as you wish*." The phrase "as you wish" is a tiny phrase, but it was enough to fire Catherine's innate love and enthusiasm for the idea of freedom. She writes: "It is here that God's boundless goodness reveals the treasure he has given to our soul, the treasure of our own free will."[11]

---

9. Pico, *Oratio*, 4–7.
10. Letter to Sano di Maco, T 69, *Le Lettere*, 1:262.
11. *Le Lettere*, 1:262.

The statement is strong by any standards. But Catherine's enthusiasm does not end there. Almost at once she lifts the phrase from its original context in Matthew's Gospel and, with an astonishing leap of insight, applies it to the actual moment of our creation. "Know," she writes, "that God said these same words to us when he created us: 'Let it be done as you wish'—that is, 'I am making you free, so that you may be subject to nothing but me.'"[12]

2. Catherine and Pico

The link between Pico's text and that of Catherine is immediately clear. And it is perhaps worth noting that Pico had developed, during his short life, close ties with the Dominican order. In fact, when he died in 1494, he was buried in the Dominican Church of San Marco in Florence, dressed in the Dominican habit. The austere Dominican reformer Girolamo Savonarola (1452–1498), a close friend of Pico, preached the sermon at his funeral, and was known to have had a notable influence on the young aristocrat, particularly on the latter part of Pico's life. The two men met and got to know one another at least four years before Pico composed his *Oratio* (1486).

Like many others in Italy at that time, Savonarola was devoted to the memory of Catherine. He made innumerable references to her in his work,[13] and he may well have shared something of this enthusiasm with Pico. As for access to Catherine's work, it's worth noting that, long before the act of formal publication, copies of her writings had been in circulation (especially in the Dominican order), passing hand to hand from one group of enthusiasts to

---

12. Letter to Sano di Maco, T 69, *Le Lettere*, 1:263.
13. See Tamar Herzig, *Savonarola's Women: Visions and Reform in Renaissance Italy* (Chicago: University of Chicago Press, 2008), 28, 31, 34.

another.[14] Is the marked similarity between Catherine's text and that of Pico merely a coincidence? Or is it possible that Pico may actually have read Catherine's letter in which the imagined conversation between Adam and the Creator was first recorded?

There is, as it happens, no hard or conclusive evidence one can find. Nevertheless, apart from the connection between Pico and Savonarola in the years prior to the composition of *Oratio*, there is another small but very interesting historical detail that could well be relevant. Pico, when studying Greek at Ferrara, became friends with Aldus Manuzio, a revered scholar of the period and the man who would eventually be responsible for editing the important second edition of St. Catherine's letters. At one point, Pico invited Aldus to tutor his two nephews at the royal house of Carpi,[15] and during the summer months of 1482, both men were together in the castle at Mirandola.[16]

Although it was a number of years before Aldus' edition of Catherine's letters appeared in 1500, it's possible that the two men—both scholars and both living in the castle at the same time—may have discussed the writings of Catherine. We do know for certain that the two men remained in contact in the years that

---

14. According to F. Thomas Luongo, "The first copies of Catherine's letters in manuscript were made by her disciples for their own meditation and education and for circulation among a network of reform-minded followers of Catherine." In other words, "Catherine's letters had circulated widely in manuscript form in the century before Aldus's edition" (Luongo, "Saintly Authorship in the Italian Renaissance: The Quattrocento Reception of Catherine of Siena's Letters," in *Catherine of Siena: The Creation of a Cult*, eds. J.E. Hamburger and G. Signori [Turnhout: Brepols, 2013], 146, 137). For further information on the first compilations of Catherine's letters, see Ragazzi, *Obeying the Truth*, 29–31.

15. See *Humanism in Fifteenth-Century Europe*, ed. David Rundle (Oxford: Medium Ævum, 2012), 339.

16. Rundle, *Humanism*, 339. See also *Pico della Mirandola: Oration on the Dignity of Man: A New Translation and Commentary*, eds. Francesco Borghesi, Michael Papio, Massimo Riva (Cambridge: Cambridge University Press, 2012), 38. Borghesi writes: "Pico spent the summer of 1482 in his castle at Mirandola, departing in the fall for Pavia."

followed. When Aldus finally published his edition of Catherine's letters, the entire enterprise was funded—and this may not be a coincidence—by Pico's sister, the Princess of Carpi. Catherine's letter containing the memorable statement voiced by the Father concerning human freedom was one of the letters included in that Venice edition.

Catherine, instead of merely talking about freedom and creation in the abstract, had come up with the ingenious idea of putting words into the mouth of the Creator. It was a bold, imaginative way of addressing the subject and, for that reason, may well have caught the eye of the young count who was himself obsessed with freedom. Certainly, if Pico did in fact read the letter, he would have remembered it. His memory for recalling texts was legendary. It was believed by his contemporaries that, if he wanted, he could recite the entire *Divine Comedy* backwards, beginning with the last line of the *Paradiso*![17]

Pico's life was short by any standard, but as an author he found time to focus attention on a truly vast range of topics.[18] Is it possible, therefore, that hidden away in one of his books relating to philosophy or theology some reference can be found to the work of Catherine of Siena? There are, it turns out, a number of explicit references to Catherine in Pico's work. All of them occur in a treatise entitled *De rerum praenotione*, and all the comments made by Pico are decidedly positive. In chapter six of book nine, Pico refers explicitly by name to the *Dialogue* of St. Catherine

---

17. Borghesi, Papio, and Riva, *Pico della Mirandola*, 905.

18. In spite of his close friendship with the Dominican friar and reformer Girolamo Savonarola, almost all of Pico's philosophical work betrays a fascination with the esoteric and represents a considerable challenge to orthodoxy. With a rare virtuoso display of learning, Pico aimed to bring into close harmony the teachings of authorities from vastly different sources, among them Plato and Aristotle, Orpheus and the Kabbalists, Averroes and Avicenna, Aquinas and Albertus Magnus, and Zoroaster and Hermes Trismegistus.

and, in that same chapter, offers what is effectively a paraphrase of *Dialogue* 71. In two of the six references he makes to Catherine, Pico places her in the company of saints and theologians such as Augustine, Dionysius, John the Anchorite, Cassian, Benedict, Dominic, and Francis. Catherine, he states, was someone "holy and blessed in heaven and honored on earth," a woman not only "accustomed to receiving divine revelations," but someone who was "experienced in discernment," and who had "committed to writing" the things she experienced in her visions.[19]

Statements of this kind, revealing a clear and intimate knowledge of Catherine's life and work, make a lot more credible the idea that Pico's celebrated paragraph on freedom may indeed have been directly influenced by the young Sienese visionary.

3. Two Visions of Freedom

If one had to choose an "anthem" or "manifesto" for the Renaissance, no text or treatise of the period could ever hope to match Pico's *Oratio*. In books, articles, lectures, and videos treating the art and sculpture of the period, it is cited again and again. That's what makes the link suggested here between Pico's text on freedom and that of Catherine so interesting. If nothing else, it alerts us to the vital connection—all too often forgotten or ignored—between medieval and Renaissance humanism. The strong, liberating words of the *Oratio*—"You can fashion yourself into whatever image you choose"—leap off the page. They are words aflame with the thought—the *dream*—of a wondrous new world of human possibility and human freedom. What they proclaim has been described by one commentator as an imperative "at once protean, libertarian, and egotistic"—a vision of life, in

---

19. Giovanni Pico della Mirandola, "De Praenotionibus discernendis," bk. 9, ch. 4, in *De rerum praenotione* (Argentorati: Knobloch, 1507).

other words, no longer pious or religious as in the past, but one entirely secular, a manifesto of a new worldliness that would in time "gird the edifice of Western individualism."[20]

That's certainly how Pico's vision came to be regarded by many students of the Renaissance years later. But Pico almost certainly never intended such a radical break with the past. Far from being doggedly secular in orientation, his vision was, if anything, intensely spiritual, and a considerable number of scholars even claim that it was mystical.[21] But the language of *Oratio* was so new, and its rhetoric of such compelling genius, that the message it communicated did indeed strike a note that to many sounded quite different from that of the great tradition. "I am making you free," the Creator had declared to Adam in Catherine's text, "so that you may be subject to nothing but me.'"[22] In Pico's text that critical phrase—"subject to nothing but me"—is not included. As a result, it might well appear that Adam is being endowed with a freedom that makes him answerable to nothing and no one. But is that the freedom Pico is proposing? Is Pico's idea that Adam can now create not merely his own place in the world and his own task but his own truth, ignoring if he wishes the truth of things as they are—even the truth of God?

Such a reading of *Oratio* does not, I believe, correspond with the plan or intention of Pico. But that plan, being articulated at

---

20. Luke Slattery, "A Renaissance Murder Mystery," *New Yorker* online, July 22, 2015, https://www.newyorker.com/culture/culture-desk/a-renaissance-murder-mystery.

21. See Francesco Borghesi, "Interpretations," in *Pico della Mirandola*, 59–60. Those commentators who focus most of their attention on the first pages of the *Oratio* are inclined to view the work as a straightforward affirmation of a new secular humanism. But to arrive at that conclusion is to ignore the impact of the full text of the work. For, apart from the opening paragraphs, the pages of the *Oratio* are marked by such a high transcendent mysticism that they represent an almost nonhuman aspiration.

22. Letter to Sano di Maco, T 69, *Le Lettere*, 1:263.

times in more visionary and poetic than academic terms, is open to misunderstanding, and for that reason can all too easily be misread as aiming to disconnect freedom from truth. Catherine, great celebrant of freedom that she was, never for a moment viewed the gift of freedom in that way. Freedom, as she saw it, was indeed something tremendous, but it was not an absolute that would permit human beings to live on earth as if they were gods, making truth the servant of their will.

That false notion, that particular reading of the *Oratio*, would in time assume the glamour of a new, popular ideology. It would, in fact, succeed in marking out a path of excitement and folly that, in the centuries after Pico, many would be drawn to pursue. Once freedom became uprooted from its ground in truth, people were inclined to make an absolute out of every form of progress and every drive for self-development, assuming at times the prerogatives of the divine themselves, and living as if all moral values were, in the end, subservient to their own individual needs and wants.

The result was progress in certain areas, even great progress. But in recent centuries, we have increasingly come to witness (in spite of many outstanding achievements in in the West) the enormous hurt—first to ourselves, and then to the environment— which this potent illusion, this godlike fantasy of unlimited and unbridled freedom and progress, has brought in its wake. Today we see all around us not a few of the tragic effects that this false understanding of freedom has wreaked on our world. We see it, for example, in the exploitation of certain parts of the developing world by the so-called free market forces of Western capitalism. And we can see it also in the absolutizing of human freedom or of human choice with respect to the life of the unborn.

What I find enormously impressive about the life and work of Catherine of Siena is that never for an instant does she give assent to the cold lie of an unreal, unlimited freedom, but rather affirms and celebrates that gift of freedom which takes flesh and form in a human way, and which seeks to recognize and defend the freedom and the desires and the needs of *others* just as much as our own. Will our contemporary postmodern society in the West recover for a new generation something of the bright, ordinary wisdom and humanity of this older vision, this premodern understanding of freedom, in the years to come?

❀

One of today's most interesting and insightful commentators on freedom is the American novelist Jonathan Franzen. When his face appeared on the front cover of *Time Magazine*, he gave an interview in which he remarked that if today our aim is to elevate freedom "to be the defining principle of what we're about as a culture and a nation, we ought to take a careful look at what freedom in practice brings."[23] Franzen, in a novel entitled *Freedom*, takes a long, careful look at the phenomenon. Reviewing the work in *Time Magazine*, Lev Grossman notes: "The weird thing about the freedom of *Freedom* is that what it doesn't bring is happiness."[24]

Franzen, reflecting on one of the central characters in his novel, remarks: "[She] had all day every day to figure out some decent and satisfactory way to live, and yet all she ever seemed to get for all her choices and all her freedom was more miserable."[25] The reviewer remarks that, at this point, Franzen is clearly going against the secular tide. "This idea," he says, "may earn Franzen

---

23. Lev Grossman, "Jonathan Franzen: The Wide Shot," *Time Magazine*, August 23, 2010, 38.
24. Grossman, "The Wide Shot," 38.
25. Grossman, "The Wide Shot," 38.

another all-American kicking."[26] But then Grossman adds: "There is something beyond freedom that people need: work, love, belief in something. Freedom is not enough. It's necessary but not sufficient. It's what you do with freedom—what you give it up for—that matters."[27]

This declaration about freedom, although it appears in a popular magazine of the twenty-first century, is one that Catherine of Siena herself could have made hundreds of years ago. What does this indicate? No more than mere coincidence, perhaps? Or is it a straw in the wind—a clear (albeit small) sign of change, pointing to an older, wiser understanding of human freedom? In this age, as in every age, freedom is not free until it opens itself up to a vision or a cause or a belief beyond itself. Freedom is not free until it serves.

---

26. Grossman, "The Wide Shot," 38.
27. Grossman, "The Wide Shot," 38. Worth setting beside this declaration are the following lines from "Spenser's Ireland" by the American poet Marianne Moore: "You're not free / until you've been made captive by / supreme belief" (*Complete Poems* [New York: Macmillan, 1991], 113).

II.
FIRE AND SHADOW: CATHERINE'S VISION OF THE SELF

INTRODUCTION TO PART II
A Path of Liberation

The pursuit of self-knowledge—a theme dominant in contemporary spirituality—was for Catherine of Siena an almost abiding fixation. Early in the *Dialogue* we hear one clear divine imperative announced to Catherine: "Never leave the knowledge of yourself!"[1] This command was one that Catherine took very much to heart. As much as, if not more than, any other author in the Christian tradition, we find her again and again insisting on the absolute necessity of attaining self-knowledge.

But if the attainment of that knowledge involves merely looking at oneself—a kind of psychological self-scrutiny—it holds no interest for Catherine. She understood from an early age that the divine command—"Never leave the knowledge of yourself"—would almost certainly be misunderstood unless another divine command, another key injunction of the Father, was obeyed—namely, "Open the eye of your mind, and look within me."[2] Catherine realized that should any of us attempt to gain knowledge of ourselves outside of God, the inevitable result would be a distorted image. But if instead we gaze into what she calls "the gentle mirror of God,"[3] we will begin at once to discover our true selves, and find, to our amazement, "the dignity and beauty"[4] of our nature.

In the present section, attention will be given to some of the different ways in which Catherine addresses another of her most

1. *Dialogue*, no. 4, 29.
2. *Dialogue*, "Prologue," 26.
3. *Dialogue*, no. 13, 48.
4. *Dialogue*, no. 13, 48.

frequent and impassioned subjects: self-knowledge in God. With regard to such knowledge, readers unfamiliar with the *Dialogue* and the *Letters* might well expect the young mystic and theologian to focus most of her attention on the innate corruption and weakness of the human being. But for Catherine, real or potential corruption is only one aspect of the self, and by no means the most important. Convinced that from the beginning human beings were made in the image and likeness of God, Catherine is inclined always to look through and beyond sin to the beauty and dignity of every individual.

The spiritual journey, once begun, will inevitably involve confrontation with "the shadow" side of oneself. Nowadays, when the subject of "the shadow" comes up for discussion, it almost always includes the name of the psychologist Carl Gustav Jung. A careful and extended comparison with Jung's teaching on the subject in Chapter Five will serve to bring into sharp focus Catherine's own understanding of "the shadow" and its role in self-knowledge. It is no small challenge to compare and contrast figures from different contexts and historical periods. Efforts of this kind tend to impose common patterns rather than disclose a more complex harmony in tension.

In this case, however, there would appear to be no risk of confusion between the two visions, since Jung tends to dismiss out of hand the medieval way of dealing with "the shadow." Can we conclude, therefore, that Jung's vision is completely at odds with that of a representative figure of the Middle Ages such as Catherine of Siena? Or is there perhaps agreement between the two authors on at least the importance of acknowledging the reality of the "shadow," and of not seeking, therefore, to avoid out of fear the challenge of what Catherine calls "the dark of self-knowledge" (*la tenebra del cognoscimento di se*)?[5]

❀

Harold Bloom, one of the best-known literary critics of our time, writes in *Ruin the Sacred Truths*: "As the years pass I develop an ever greater horror of solitude, of finding myself having to confront sleepless nights and baffled days in which the self ceases to know how to talk to itself."[6] It is an honest and rather startling admission, and I have a sense that, in some measure at least, it speaks for a generation. But is there an answer to this not uncommon dilemma? I am persuaded that, as much as any other teaching on the subject, whether ancient or modern, Catherine of Siena's reflections on self-knowledge offer a genuine path of liberation, a way of overcoming that fear of inner solitude of which Bloom speaks.

---

5. Letter to the Prior and Brothers of the Company of the Virgin Mary, T 184, *Letters*, 2:311. For the original Italian text, see *Le Lettere*, 3:117.

6. Harold Bloom, *Ruin the Sacred Truths* (Cambridge, MA: Harvard University Press, 1991), 131.

CHAPTER 4
"Who Am I?":
Catherine and Self-Knowledge

"Who am I?" This question was at the heart of Catherine of Siena's spiritual journey. But Catherine was not, it goes without saying, the first author in the Christian tradition to explore in depth the question of identity. The whole issue had already been addressed many times in the writings of celebrated authors like St. Augustine of Hippo and St. Bernard of Clairvaux.[1] Catherine, because of her lack of learning, was prevented from directly reading the writings of these authors—books, homilies, treatises, etc.—but *indirectly* she would have imbibed their influence, being able, over many years, to enjoy regular contact with nuns, hermits, preachers, and ascetics, and experiencing a variety of monastic and religious traditions in and around Siena.

These men and women religious were manifestly important sources. But the most immediate influence, the real fountain and source of Catherine's teaching on this particular topic, came not from something outside—not from an *external* source—but sprang from within, from her own profound knowledge of self. This knowledge has two very different, very distinctive aspects. On the one hand, Catherine discovered with contemplative joy that she was created out of love, formed in the very image and likeness of God. On the other hand, she discovered, through her practice of prayer and from the experience of day-to-day living,

---

1. Over many centuries, of course, this question of self-knowledge had already been addressed by religious thinkers and philosophers—in the Veda, for example, and in the writings of Confucius, Plato, and Aristotle.

that at times she could be stubborn and self-willed, and was often inclined to be harsh in her judgment of others. In one letter she speaks of what she calls "my lack of charity"[2] and in another of "my stunted life."[3] And in a prayer at Avignon, addressing God the Father, she confesses:

> I am a foolish and wretched creature while you are supreme goodness. I am death and you are life. I am darkness and you are light. I am ignorance and you are wisdom. You are infinite and I am finite. I am sick and you are the doctor. I am a weak sinner who has never loved you.[4]

An open and honest acknowledgment of past failure was, for Catherine, of fundamental importance in the spiritual life. At no stage, however, did she suggest that we are obliged, with grim repetitiveness, to put our face down into the mud of the memory of our past sin. Accordingly, to a contemplative nun who was suffering greatly from discouragement, she wrote:

> I really want you to see your nothingness and negligence and ignorance—but I don't want you to see them through the darkness of discouragement but in the light of the infinite goodness of God that you find within yourself. Understand that the devil would like nothing better than to have you go over and over the knowledge of your wretchedness without anything else to season it. But that knowledge has to be seasoned with hope in God's mercy.[5]

---

2. Letter to Francesco di Pipino, T 265, *Letters*, 4:87.
3. Letter to Raymond of Capua, T 344, *Letters*, 4:231.
4. Prayer 1, *Prayers*, 8–9.
5. Letter to Suor Costanza, T 73, *Letters*, 1:305–306.

1. "In the Gentle Mirror of God": Freedom and Contemplative Prayer

According to Catherine, in order to discover who and what we are in any kind of depth, we need not only to look within ourselves but also to lift our gaze above and beyond ourselves. "In your nature, eternal Godhead, I shall come to know my nature. And what is my nature, boundless Love? It is fire, because you are nothing but a fire of love."[6] The journey towards true self-knowledge requires that we see ourselves directly under the gaze of the One who created us. "In the gentle mirror of God," Catherine writes, the believer when at prayer "sees her own dignity: that through no merit of hers but by his creation she is the image of God."[7] That said, however, what the believer discovers, in this act of gazing, is by no means all brightness and consolation. In "the mirror of continual prayer,"[8] Catherine explains, she begins to see her faults and failures far more clearly than ever before. "In the mirror of God's goodness she sees as well her own unworthiness, the work of her own sin."[9]

This humbling discovery is the inevitable result of being now able to contemplate even a little the wonderful innocence and purity of the Godhead. "For just as you can better see the blemish on your face when you look at yourself in a mirror, so the soul who in true self-knowledge rises up with desire to look at herself in the gentle mirror of God . . . sees all the more clearly her own defects because of the purity she sees in him."[10] Catherine, in the *Dialogue*, describes her own experience of self-knowledge in God

---

6. Prayer 12, *Prayers*, 117.
7. *Dialogue*, no. 13, 48.
8. Letter to Rainaldo da Capua, T 343, *Letters*, 4:268.
9. *Dialogue*, no. 13, 48.
10. *Dialogue*, no. 13, 48.

as both "sweet" and "bitter." At one point, referring to herself in the third person, she writes: "Now as light and knowledge grew more intense in this soul, a sweet bitterness was both heightened and mellowed."[11] *Bitter* because Catherine could now recognize, as never before, her capacity for failure, but also *sweet* because that very acknowledgement served to heighten her awareness of the loving kindness and mercy of the Father.

❀

One vital thread running through all of Catherine's work is her belief that without the saving but demanding truth that self-knowledge brings, there can be no real freedom. What is required of us, Catherine explains, is that we undergo what she calls "the night of self-knowledge."[12] Without that humble, purifying knowledge, we will have no protection against our enemies, and we will find ourselves enslaved by things such as "pride" and "presumption," "passion and worldly pleasure."[13] But if instead we enter willingly into that "night," we will in time have the experience of a new "dawn," and "the sun will rise and give us a bright day."[14] Catherine is writing here to Stefano Maconi, a young friend and disciple of whom she was particularly fond. "Think of it, dearest son. You'll never be captured as long as you are living in the night of true self-knowledge. . . . I want you always to live between day and night by coming to know yourself in God and God in yourself."[15]

Catherine is aware that there are many kinds of battles to be fought and challenges to be overcome in the spiritual life. And

---

11. *Dialogue*, no. 13, 48.
12. Letter to Stefano Maconi, T 365, *Letters*, 3:134.
13. *Letters*, 3:134.
14. *Letters*, 3:133–134.
15. *Letters*, 3:133.

certain virtues such as "patience, courage, and perseverance" will be needed along the way if progress is to be made.[16] But how in practice are they to be acquired? "These virtues," Catherine writes, "have their wellspring in self-knowledge."[17] For it is in the struggle to overcome weaknesses of all kinds—when "I would free myself from these things"[18]—that I discover the true depth of my need, and arrive at the realization that, without the help of grace, "I cannot free myself."[19] Only then, in light of that humble knowledge, can I begin in significant measure to acquire the virtues. Catherine's point is clear: the journey we hope to make from bondage to freedom, from vice to virtue, from weakness to strength—if it is to prove successful—must from the beginning take care not to avoid or ignore the challenge of "true self-knowledge."[20]

2. "Do You Know Who You Are?"

Catherine, during the countless hours she spent at prayer and meditation, was told wondrous things about the dignity and beauty of her own nature, and indeed about human nature in general. But on one occasion, when she was alone in her "cell" at Siena, she received a message from God that, at first hearing, seemed to

---

16. Letter to Don Cristofano, T 335, *Letters*, 2:584.
17. *Letters*, 2:584.
18. *Letters*, 2:584.
19. *Letters*, 2:584.
20. Catherine, writing to her niece Nanna and reflecting on the question of freedom and self-knowledge, speaks of the virtue of patience and, along with it, what she calls "that dear little virtue, profound humility." "But," she writes, "we cannot attain this virtue of humility except through true self-knowledge. I mean we must know our own poverty and weakness, that of ourselves we are incapable of a single virtuous act or of freeing ourselves from any pain or struggle" (Letter to Nanna, T 23, *Letters*, 2:558. See also Letter to Francesco di Bartolomeo de' Casini, T 244, *Letters*, 3:34).

contradict all the affirmative things she had been told up to that point. According to the report given by Raymond of Capua, God said to Catherine: "Do you know, daughter, who you are and who I am? . . . You are she who is not, and I AM HE WHO IS."[21]

These two statements, far from being calculated to make Catherine feel that she counted for nothing in the eyes of God, were intended, Raymond tells us, as nothing less than "a betrothal-pledge."[22] Acceptance by Catherine of their meaning, their import, would set her feet "on the royal road which leads to the fullness of grace, and truth, and light."[23] Catherine would have "beatitude" in her grasp.[24] Well, that does indeed sound reassuring! But viewed from the perspective of common sense and reason, what light or truth or grace—what *beatitude*—could possibly be based on the words addressed to Catherine: "You are she who is not"?

As an aid towards unravelling this puzzling conundrum, there is in the *Dialogue* one passage that merits close attention. Catherine, after stating openly, "I am she who is not," addresses God the Father: "You alone are who you are, and whatever being I have and every other gift of mine I have from you."[25] So utterly convinced is Catherine of her complete dependence on God that she confesses in the same passage: "If I should claim to be anything of myself, I should be lying through my teeth!"[26] These are strong and bold assertions, but they do not exhaust the full meaning of the statements made originally to Catherine. For it soon becomes clear that, at their core, they are nothing less than a revelation of love.

21. *Life*, no. 10, 85.
22. *Life*, no. 10, 89.
23. *Life*, no. 10, 85.
24. *Life*, no. 10, 85.
25. *Dialogue*, no. 134, 273–274.
26. *Dialogue*, no. 134, 273.

Responding on one occasion to the question of how in practice people come to the realization that they are loved by God, Catherine replied, "In holy self-knowledge . . . we see that we were loved before we came into existence, for God's love for us compelled him to create us."[27] The idea is startling. That something or someone, a mere "nothing," could be loved into existence and most tenderly held there by God, is a stupendous thought, a thing of wonder—and it is the hidden, joyous meaning of "You are she who is not."

In Raymond's *Legenda maior,* the statement "You are she who is not" is taken up and looked at from many different angles. Although small, the phrase contains, Raymond declares, "a meaning without limit" and "a wisdom without measure."[28] He writes: "Let us take the trouble to unearth it, for even what we see on the surface shows that a rich hoard lies hidden here."[29] What is that hidden wisdom, that buried "hoard"? It is, he tells us, the revelation of a "bountiful and gracious Lord . . . who loves his creatures so much, and bears them such good will, that they were loved by him before he ever made them."[30]

These lines of Raymond are indeed very fine. But on the subject of self-knowledge, nothing quite measures up to Catherine's illumined thoughts and expressions. Her words impact the reader like radiant arrows. They strike with force; her voice comes to us as wholly alive and wholly present. On one occasion, addressing head-on the question of the "nothing" in self-knowledge, she writes: "I have no doubt that if you turn your understanding's eye to look at yourself and realize that you are not, you will discover

---

27. Letter to Monna Lodovica di Granello, T 304, *Letters,* 3:185.
28. *Life,* no. 92, 85.
29. *Life,* no. 93, 86.
30. *Life,* no. 96, 88.

with what blazing love your being has been given to you. I tell you, your heart and affection will not be able to keep from exploding for love."[31]

3. Freedom in Love: The Drama of
Attachment and Detachment

Certain passages in the *Dialogue* reflect on the ordinary but vivid drama of human affection, how the attention of an individual can become focused on another person "with a special love," and how this deep attachment can in time become the occasion of acquiring certain basic self-knowledge. According to the *Dialogue*, this love, this attachment, can either develop into a friendship that's wholly positive or into a relationship that's far from perfect. "Do you know," the Father says to Catherine, "how you can tell when your spiritual love is not perfect? If you are distressed when it seems that those you love are not returning your love or not loving you as much as you think you love them. Or if you are distressed when it seems to you that you are being deprived of their company or comfort, or that they love someone else more than you."[32]

Here what is being judged as problematic is not the emotion of the reaction itself—for that's to be expected—but rather the possessive character of the love behind the emotion. If love is indeed based on no more than the fulfillment of one's own need for the presence of the other, and if that is all that "special love" means, the end result, the Father explains to Catherine, is probable suffering and distress. "Whenever the soul loves someone with

---

31. Letter to a Great Prelate, T 16, *Letters*, 2:116.
32. *Dialogue*, no. 64, 121.

a special love, she feels pain when the pleasure or comfort or companionship she has become accustomed to, and which gave her great consolation, is lessened. Or she suffers if she sees that person keeping more company with someone else than with her."[33]

But things don't end there—at least, not necessarily. Against all expectation, this negative, unhappy experience can yield a positive result: "This pain," the Father observes, "makes her enter into knowledge of herself."[34] Elsewhere in the *Dialogue*, addressing Catherine directly, the Father declares, "This is why I often permit you to form such a love, so that you may come through it to know yourself."[35] What is being stated here is of tremendous importance. Catherine, in the process of attaining self-knowledge, had to struggle—not just once or twice, but *often*—with the question of her attachment to certain individuals among her friends and associates.

Catherine's letters betray again and again the depth of her affection for certain individuals, and the consequent risk she must have faced of becoming over-attached. "Of ourselves," she admits in one place, "we are frail and weak where our sensual selves are concerned, especially when we love ourselves very much and when we love other people and material possessions in a sensual way. If we love them so much, with a clinging and sensual love, then we suffer intolerable pain when we lose them later on."[36] How to answer this dilemma? The solution, as Catherine sees it, is first and last to find our strength in God, and then to do everything we can "to subdue our weakness with reason, with willpower, and with the hand of free choice."[37]

---

33. *Dialogue*, no. 144, 302.
34. *Dialogue*, no. 144, 302.
35. *Dialogue*, no. 64, 121.
36. Letter to Marco Bindi, T 13, *Letters*, 4:16.
37. *Letters*, 4:16.

In one of her letters, addressing the question of "inordinate love," she writes: "We are always forming attachments. As soon as God cuts off one branch from under us, we grab onto another."[38] The honest, sharp-edged character of this remark, and others like it, may possibly indicate something of the struggle Catherine herself had to undergo in order to be free from certain attachments. It's not inconceivable, therefore, that a few of the saint's hard sayings on the subject—for example, "Cut yourself free in every respect from these bonds"[39]—may have been addressed originally, and with the same bold and direct challenge, to Catherine herself.

What, then, are we to conclude? In the opinion of St. Catherine, is it always a mistake to allow a "special love" for another person to develop and flourish? Is the strong bond of affection that can exist between two people something to be discouraged in our pursuit of perfection? Fortunately, this is not at all what Catherine is proposing. In the first place, she has every confidence that, should a particular love be in any way "disordered" or imperfect, it can with the help of grace and human effort be transformed into "well-ordered love."[40] She herself on occasion appears by no means unwilling to acknowledge a disordered attachment. But Catherine's principal concern is always with finding a way forward. "I was deluded," she writes to Raymond of Capua, "when I looked for [satisfaction] in other people. So in times of loneliness I want to find companionship in the blood."[41] By "blood" Catherine means, of course, the unconditional love of God made manifest in Jesus—specifically, her own profound experience of

---

38. Letter to Madonna Biancina, T 111, *Le Lettere*, 2:159.
39. Letter to Peronella, T 360, *Letters*, 4:252. In a letter to Raymond, Catherine writes: "Free yourself from every creature—of me first of all" (T 102, *Letters*, 4:348).
40. *Dialogue*, no. 144, 302.
41. Letter to Raymond, T 102, *Letters*, 4:348.

that love. "In this way," she continues, "I will find both the blood and these other people, and in the blood I will drink their love and affection."[42]

By the illumination and purifying grace of what Catherine calls the "blood," not only is the contemplative led into the bright humble realm of self-knowledge, but she is also afforded the joy of deep and close companionship—first with Christ, and then with the friend whom she loves with a "special love." In the *Dialogue* we read:

> If she is willing to walk wisely in the light as she ought, she will come to love that special person more perfectly, for with self-knowledge and the contempt she has conceived for her selfish feelings, she will cast off imperfection and come to perfection. . . . For I [God the Father] have permitted the struggles and the special love and everything else to bring her to the light of perfection.[43]

❀

One of the friends on whom Catherine bestowed a "special love" was a young man from the minor nobility of Siena called Stefano Maconi. Of the same age as Catherine, he was by all accounts a singularly attractive and lovable individual. Struck by the great peace and joy he experienced when in her company, Stefano decided to join Catherine's *famiglia* early in 1376.[44] He became one of her most devoted secretaries. "She loved me," he writes,

---

42. Letter to Raymond, T 102, *Letters*, 4:348. In another place Catherine speaks without hesitation of the "special intimate love" between herself and Raymond, distinguishing it from "the love we should have in general for every person"

(T 344, *Letters*, 4:230).

43. *Dialogue*, no. 144, 302–303.

44. Before 1376, Stefano was not interested in meeting someone like Catherine. "At that time," he writes, "I was completely immersed in the currents of worldly living, but Eternal Goodness . . . arranged through this virgin to free my soul from the jaws of hell" ("Il Processo Castellano," *Fontes Vitae S. Catharinae Senensis Historici*, 9:258–259).

"with the tenderness of a mother, far more than I deserved. . . . She admitted me into her closest confidence."[45] In the spring of 1376, Stefano was asked by Catherine to travel with her to the papal palace at Avignon. That journey was to be one of several that he made with Catherine outside Siena.

The prolonged absence of Stefano away from home caused his mother, Monna Giovanna, much heartbreak. In the end she voiced her complaint, and her sad lament reached the ears of Catherine. The letter that Catherine wrote to Monna in reply in November of 1376 is an astonishing epistle.[46] It betrays not the least hint of hesitation or shyness about her "special love" for Stefano. On the contrary, by a rather brilliant and dexterous sleight of hand, Catherine effectively claims Stefano as her own. She writes:

> Do not be disturbed that I have kept Stefano so long, for I have taken good care of him. By love and by affection I have become one with him, and so I have treated your things as if they were my own. I think you have not taken this in bad part. I want to do all I can for you, and for him, even up to death. You, mother, bore him once; and I wish to bear him and you and all your family in tears and in sweat by continual prayers and desire for your salvation.[47]

By love and by affection I have become one with him. The statement is decidedly bold. It leaves us in no doubt about the depth and quality of St. Catherine's "special love" for her young friend

---

45. Letter of Stefano Maconi to Tommaso d'Antonio (Caffarini), cited in Augusta T. Drane, *History of St. Catherine of Siena and Her Companions* (London: Burns and Oates, 1880), 294. When Catherine died, Stefano carried her body to the Minerva. And it was Stefano, at the end, who with his own hands laid the body of Catherine in its coffin of cypress wood, reverently kissing it and weeping profusely.

46. Letter to Monna Giovanna di Corrado Maconi, T 247, *Le Lettere*, vol. 4 (Florence: Giunti, 1940), 58. A few months earlier Catherine sent another letter to Monna, Stefano's mother.

47. *Le Lettere*, 4:58.

and devoted disciple. Both of them, as it happens, were together at Avignon in August 1376. There, on the Vigil of the Assumption, Catherine, while absorbed in an ecstasy of contemplation, was overheard by those in attendance speaking with God at great length. Her prayer concluded with these words:

> I pray to you also
> for all the children you have given me
> to love with a special love
> through your boundless charity,
> most high, eternal, ineffable Godhead.
> Amen.

4. Self-Hatred and Self-Love: Finding the Gospel Path

When talking with others, Catherine was always candid about her own "defects." "Wretch that I am," she confessed, "I've so often fallen into unhappiness and into passing judgment on my neighbors."[48] And again: "I am not so virtuous as to know how to do anything but imperfectly."[49] Such admissions of weakness— although at times, no doubt, greatly exaggerated ("My own sins are numberless," she declared on one occasion[50])—are nevertheless admissions that spring from feelings of real sorrow and real regret.

The fact of recurrent failure and the painful recognition of radical weakness can breed, in the lives of certain individuals, emotions of both shame and self-hatred. If by "shame" here is understood the honest admission of failure and the unhappy

---

48. Letter to Daniella of Orvieto, T 65, *Letters*, 3:240.

49. Letter to the Lord Defenders of the City of Siena, T 121, *Letters*, 2:416. In a letter to Raymond of Capua we hear Catherine exclaim: "My love is lukewarm. . . . Woe is me, my Lord! Will I be like this always and everywhere and in every situation?" (Letter to Raymond, T 344, *Letters*, 4:229).

50. Letter to Biringhieri degli Arzocchi, T 24, *Letters*, 2:158.

feelings that accompany it, that would not be strange. But actual "self-hatred"? Under any rubric, or title, or understanding, can that ever be the response to human weakness that the great Catholic spiritual tradition actively recommends?

On this subject, Catherine's approach merits close attention. Although she does appear on occasion to support an attitude of self-dislike or even self-hatred, what she is concerned to uphold is not a cold disdain of self but rather a whole-hearted hatred of the slavery of sin, something that mocks the self and mocks all hope of freedom. Writing in an early letter to the poet Neri dei Pagliaresi, Catherine speaks approvingly of what she calls "the sword of self-hatred and self-contempt."[51] This statement, if read or understood in the wrong way, could certainly be dangerous. Fortunately, Catherine makes clear that what she has in mind here is *not* disdain of one's own being, but rather what she calls "hatred and contempt of sin."[52] Elsewhere Catherine draws our attention to the distinction between a false love of self on the one hand, and an enlightened love of self on the other, noting with regret how people tend to love "whatever agrees with that puny sensual part of themselves *rather than loving themselves reasonably.*"[53]

Catherine, along with many of the great spiritual authors in the tradition, writes with urgency about the dangers of false self-love. But with no less urgency, she writes also about the dangers of cold self-hate. Catherine knows that many of those who attempt to follow a spiritual path can easily become, as a result of repeated failure, harsh in their judgment of their own being. Of those closest to Catherine, the individual who most stands out in this regard is Neri, a man much given to melancholy and self-torment. He was

---

51. Letter to Neri dei Pagliaresi, T 99, *Letters*, 1:14.
52. *Letters*, 1:15.
53. Letter to Cardinal Iacopo Orsini, T 223, *Letters*, 2:162 (emphasis added).

constantly at risk, as a result, of falling into what Catherine called (in the original Italian) "*confusione.*"

How best to translate this word? If considered at the level of the mind, it refers to a state of mental self-doubt and grim self-interrogation; at the level of the heart, to a deep and wounding sense of discouragement. Catherine writes to Neri: "I want all your *confusione* to be burned up and to disappear in the trust in the blood, in the fire of God's boundless charity. Let nothing remain but true knowledge of yourself."[54] Then she goes on to say with even greater eloquence:

> Isn't God more ready to forgive than we are to sin? And isn't he our doctor—and we the sick ones? Isn't he the bearer of our iniquities? And doesn't he consider spiritual discouragement [*la confusione della mente*] worse than any other sin? Yes indeed! So, dearest son, open your mind's eye with its light, most holy faith, and see how much God loves you. Don't become discouraged [*non entrare in confusione*] as you consider his love and your heart's coldness but let the fire of holy desire grow in true knowledge and humility.[55]

What Catherine calls *confusione* has the effect of stirring up in the heart of the individual a kind of self-loathing. Not only, she explains, is it "a leprosy that dries up soul and body and keeps us in continual torment," it also "makes us unbearable even to ourselves."[56] The letter to Neri concludes: "With living faith, then, and with holy desire and firm trust in [Christ's] blood, let the devil of discouragement [*confusione*] be vanquished. I'll say no more. Keep living in God's holy and tender love. I beg God to give you his gentle blessing. Gentle Jesus. Jesus, love!"[57]

---

54. Letter to Neri dei Pagliaresi, T 178, *Letters*, 4:263.
55. *Letters*, 4:263.
56. *Letters*, 4:264.
57. *Letters*, 4:264.

In early May 1376, moved by the same spirit of kindness and concern, Catherine addresses once again the unhappy phenomenon of self-torment and self-disdain in a letter to Suor Costanza. She speaks of "the darkness of unwarranted despondency [*disordinata confusione*] that often enters the soul under the guise and pretext of a stupid sort of humility."[58] Then she goes on to explain what she means exactly by *confusione*:

> I mean when notions come into the heart that say, "What you are doing is neither pleasing nor acceptable to God; you are in a state of damnation." And little by little, after these notions have caused discouragement, they infiltrate the soul and point out a way disguised as humility, saying, "You can see that because of your sins you aren't worthy of many graces and gifts"—and so the person stays away from communion and from other spiritual gifts and practices. This is the devil's trick, the darkness he causes.[59]

5. Darkness into Light: The Path of Illumination

"Darkness" is the word Catherine uses most often, and with most insistence, when she speaks of the Evil One. The devil's aim, she explains, is to invade the mind "with shadows,"[60] breeding as much confusion as possible and undermining, by use of subtle temptation and whispered lies, the individual's sense of integrity and self-worth. The solution, as Catherine sees it, is to open our mind and heart to the light of God's compassion—something that we hear repeated by Catherine many times in her writings. But on occasion we also hear Catherine speaking directly to God in exactly the way she recommends to others. Reflecting, for example, on the mystery of divine compassion and divine light,

58. Letter to Suor Costanza, T 73, *Letters*, 1:305.
59. *Letters*, 1:305.
60. Letter to Frate Antonio of Nizza, T 17, *Le Lettere*, 1:58.

and stressing the importance in the act of contemplation of a free and committed engagement of the human will, Catherine says to the Father:

> If we open the eye of our understanding with a will to know you, we know you, for your light enters into every soul who opens the gate of her will. For the light stands at the soul's gate, and as soon as the gate is opened to it, the light enters, just like the sun that knocks at the shuttered window and, as soon as it is opened, comes into the house. So the soul has to have a will to know, and with that will she has to open her understanding's eye, and then you, true Sun, enter the soul and flood her with the light that is yourself. And once you have entered, what do you do, Light of Compassion, within the soul? You dispel the darkness and give her light. You draw out of her the dampness of selfish love and leave her the fire of your charity. You make her heart free, for in your light she has come to know what great liberty you have given us by snatching us from slavery to the devil. . . . She closes her will so that it loves nothing outside of you but loves you above all things and everything in you according to your will and wants only to follow you. Then she is truly compassionate to herself, and just as she is compassionate to herself, so is she to her neighbors, ready to give up her bodily life for the salvation of souls. In all things she exercises compassion wisely because she has seen how wisely you have worked all your mysteries in us.[61]

There is one brief statement made in that quotation that is startling in its implication but that could easily be passed over unnoticed—namely, "the light stands at the soul's gate." What this means is that the "true Sun," the light of the divinity, will not enter and flood the soul with light unless the soul accepts to open to him the eye of its understanding. Here one is reminded

---

61. Prayer 15, *Prayers*, 153–154.

of Catherine's description of the event of the Annunciation, that decisive encounter between heaven and earth in which "human strength and freedom are revealed."[62] Also laid bare by this event is the manifest respect that God has for human freedom. Catherine—moved no doubt by the unexpected display of divine humility and by the simple courage of Mary's *fiat*—turns to the young mother and exclaims: "God's Son did not come down into your womb until you had given your will's consent. He waited at the door of your will to open to him."[63]

6. Self-Knowledge in God: Nine Images

Catherine, when addressing the question of self-knowledge in God, refers again and again to nine central images: the cell, the fountain, the peaceful sea, the tomb, the stable, the night, the well, the full circle, and the house. Of all of the images, "the cell" is the image that Catherine employs most often. Right at the start of the *Dialogue* we are informed that Catherine had "become accustomed to dwelling in the cell of self-knowledge."[64]

i. The Cell

"This cell," she explains to a close friend, "is really two rooms in one."[65] The first room offers the joyful knowledge of being loved by God; the second room, in contrast, offers the painful knowledge of human weakness. But both rooms, Catherine makes clear, need to be inhabited at the same time, "otherwise your soul would end

---

62. Prayer 18, *Prayers*, 192. For Catherine's brief prayerful reflection on the Annunciation, see pages 27–28 above.
63. Prayer 18, *Prayers*, 192.
64. *Dialogue*, no. 1, 25.
65. Letter to Mona Alessa dei Saracini, T 49, *Letters*, 2:601.

up either in confusion [discouragement and self-doubt] or in presumption."[66]

Writing to another correspondent, Suor Costanza, and once again taking up the image of the cell, Catherine writes: "Do you know how you ought to act? Just as you do when you go to your cell at night to sleep. . . . It is clear that you need your cell [that is, basic knowledge of self], but your cell isn't all you need."[67] At this point, Catherine imagines the nun glancing over at the bed in her cell. The bed, needless to say, stands for more than simple repose. For Catherine, it represents absolute security in the knowledge of being loved by God. And so, with a burst of playful exuberance, she declares to Costanza: "Walk across the cell and get into bed, the bed in which is God's tender goodness, which you find within this cell, yourself."[68]

Catherine, in her enthusiasm at this point, begins to mix metaphors, and to an almost alarming degree: "In this bed," she writes, "there is food, table, and waiter. The Father is table for you; the Son is your food; the Holy Spirit waits on you. And the same Holy Spirit makes of himself a bed for you. . . . I beg you, then, for love of Christ crucified, stay in this lovely, glorious restful bed."[69]

ii. The Fountain

Another favorite image of Catherine's is the fountain. Referring in one place to Christ as "the fountain of First Truth," she writes: "At this fountain you will discover your soul's dignity."[70] Elsewhere, in a similar vein, Catherine describes how, by gazing at our reflection in "the wellspring [fonte] of the sea of the divine

---

66. Letter to Mona Alessa dei Saracini, T 49, Letters, 2:602.
67. Letter to Suor Costanza, T 73, Letters, 1:306.
68. Letters, 1:306.
69. Letters, 1:306.
70. Letter to Monna Melina, T 164, Letters, 2:31.

Essence,"[71] we gain knowledge of both our human wretchedness and our human dignity, for "we see neither our dignity nor the defects that mar the beauty of our soul unless we go and look at ourselves in the still sea of the divine Essence wherein we are portrayed; for from it we came when God's Wisdom created us to his image and likeness."[72] And so she concludes: "Let us go, then, to the fountain of God's sweet goodness. There we shall discover the knowledge of ourselves and of God. And when we dip our vessel in, we shall draw out the water of divine grace, powerful enough to give us everlasting life."[73]

iii. The Peaceful Sea

In 1375 Catherine travelled from Pisa to its port at Livorno in 1375—an experience that had a powerful impact on her. "I have just rediscovered the sea," she wrote, "not that the sea is new, but it is new to me in the way my soul experiences it."[74] Stunned by the great beauty of what she witnessed, she began from that time on to refer to God as a "peaceful sea" (*mare pacifico*). In a letter to Raymond, for example, Catherine writes: "There is no other way we can either see our dignity or the faults that mar our soul's beauty, except by going to look into the quiet sea of the divine Being. There, in that Being, we see our reflection. Why? Because we came forth from there when God's wisdom created us in God's image and likeness."[75]

When in the *Dialogue* Catherine comes to reflect on the illumined knowledge of self that comes with living faith, she

---

71. Letter to Raymond, T 226, *I, Catherine*, 171.
72. *I, Catherine*, 172.
73. Letter to Monna Melina, T 164, *Letters*, 2:32.
74. Letter to Frate Bartolomeo Dominici, T 146, *Letters*, 1:96.
75. Letter to Raymond of Capua, T 226, *Letters*, 2:8.

speaks of faith as "a sea" whose water, she says, is a "mirror."[76] "When I look into this mirror, holding it in the hand of love, it shows me myself, as your creation, in you, and you in me though the union you have brought about of the Godhead with our humanity."[77] The two images of a mirror and the sea are both present in the letter that Catherine wrote after her visit to the port of Livorno. So profound was the experience that day of gazing out at the *mare pacifico*, it made Catherine think of the words "God is love." And this in turn prompted her to compose the following bright and thoughtful meditation:

> Just as the sun shines its light on the earth and a mirror reflects a person's face, so these words echo within me that everything that is done is simply love, because everything is made entirely of love. This is why he says, "I am God, Love." This sheds light on the priceless mystery of the incarnate Word, who, out of sheer love, was given in such humility that it confounds my pride. It teaches us to look not just at what he did, but at the blazing love this Word has given us. It says that we should do what a loving person does when a friend comes with a gift, not looking at the friend's hands to see what the gift is, but looking with the eyes of love at the friend's loving heart. And this is what God's supreme, eternal, more tender than tender goodness wants us to do when he visits our soul.[78]

iv. The Tomb

Of all the images for self-knowledge in God employed by Catherine, perhaps the most vivid and most unexpected is that

---

76. *Dialogue*, no. 167, 365.
77. *Dialogue*, no. 167, 365–366.
78. Letter to Frate Bartolomeo Dominici, T 146, *Letters*, 1:96.

of "the tomb of self-knowledge." We find the image taken up by Catherine and developed most memorably in a letter that she sent to a young monk or friar who had abandoned religious life. First of all, Catherine appeals to him to return to his monastery: "Oh dearest son, turn your memory back a bit. Open your mind's eye to recognize your sins in hope of mercy. See the truth! Return to your fold!"[79] As soon as he returns to his community, to "the fold" to which he belongs, he will, Catherine assures him, find out the truth, since then he will be "free from sin."[80] The truth for Catherine is, of course, nothing other than God's mercy: "In this mercy," she writes, "you will find relief from the terrible dejection that seems to have come from seeing yourself fallen from the heights of heaven into profound and total misery."[81] So she goes on to say: "Hide yourself under the wings of God's mercy, for he is more ready to pardon than you are to sin."[82]

Towards the end of the letter, in one particular paragraph, Catherine takes up the theme of self-knowledge. Here, she not only explores the traditional Christian images of death and resurrection in a way that is totally original, but also—prompted, it would appear, by her natural kindness and by a keen and thoughtful intuition—finds a strong, imaginative way of drawing the young man, clearly burdened by guilt, into the grace and promise of the Paschal Mystery. She writes:

> Go into the tomb of self-knowledge, and with Magdalen ask, "Who will roll back the stone from the tomb for me? For the stone (that is, the guilt of sin) is so heavy that I can't budge it." And as soon as you have acknowledged and confessed how imperfect and heavy you are, you will see two angels, who will roll this stone

---

79. Letter to a Brother who has left his Order, T 173, *Letters*, 2:512.
80. *Letters*, 2:512.
81. *Letters*, 2:512.
82. *Letters*, 2:512.

away. I mean that divine help will send you the angel of holy love and reverence for God (a love that is never alone but gives us the company of love for our neighbors), and the angel of hatred [for sin] (accompanied by true humility and patience), to roll this stone away. So, with true hope and lively faith, never leave the tomb of self-knowledge. Persevere in staying there until you find Christ risen in your soul by grace. Once you have found him, go and proclaim it to your brothers—and your brothers are the true, solid, lovely virtues with whom you want to and do take up your residence. Then, Christ lets you touch him in continual humble prayer by appearing to your soul in a way you can feel.[83]

v. The Stable

With regard to the attainment of self-knowledge, Catherine refers on occasion to the example of the saints—to St. Mary Magdalene, for example, and to others.[84] But on a few rare occasions, she refers also to Christ. In one of her prayers, addressing Christ directly, she says very simply and very clearly: "You understood yourself."[85] Though brief, this statement, in light of the divine and human natures of Christ, carries quite an extraordinary weight of significance. It prompts Catherine to ask a question: "What, then, was your glory, oh gentle loving Word? You yourself. For you had to suffer in order to enter into your very self."[86] With regard to the witness given to us by the incarnate Word, God the Father says in the *Dialogue*:

> He taught you not only with words but by his example as well, from his birth right up to the end of his life. . . . You see this gentle loving Word born in a stable while Mary was on a journey, to

---

83. Letter to a Brother who has left his Order, T 173, *Letters*, 2:512.

84. See Letter to Monna Bartolomea, T 42, *Letters*, 2:42. See also Letter to Frate Matteo di Francisco Tolomei, T 94, *Letters*, 2:672.

85. Oratio XIII, *S. Caterina da Siena: Le Orazioni*, 164.

86. *Le Orazioni*, 164.

show you pilgrims how you should be constantly born anew in the stable of self-knowledge, where by grace you will find me within your soul. You see him lying among the animals, in such poverty that Mary had nothing to cover him up with. It was winter, and she kept him warm with the animals' breath and a blanket of hay. He is the fire of charity but he chose to endure the cold in his humanity. All his life long he chose to suffer. . . . He was nailed to the cross to loose you from the chains of deadly sin. By becoming a servant he rescued you from slavery to the devil and set you free.[87]

vi. The Night

"Try to get to know yourself!" Catherine makes this appeal to Raymond in a letter in which she speaks about what she calls "the night of self-knowledge."[88] Night—a demanding period of spiritual darkness—descended on Catherine at the close of a three-year period of solitude and seclusion. She was about twenty years old. While in solitude she had been blessed with a number of quite remarkable illuminations, and she had experienced also the radiantly felt presence of her divine Lord and Master. All that changed, however, when it seemed that the God with whom she had enjoyed such intimacy was now completely abandoning her. According to Raymond, "Her Spouse who up till now had been accustomed to visit her frequently and fill her with his consolations, seemed to withdraw."[89] The young Catherine was devastated. "Her soul," Raymond writes, "was plunged in a very

87. *Dialogue*, no. 151, 320.
88. Letter to Raymond of Capua, T 104, *Letters*, 2:654.
89. *Life*, no. 107, 99. This experience, often referred to as "the dark night," is described most memorably in the work of the Carmelite mystic St. John of the Cross. Catherine only once, to my knowledge, cites the actual phrase itself. It occurs in the long Passion Sunday prayer of 1379. In a spirit of deep humility, Catherine says to God the Father: "If I gaze into your exaltedness, any rising up to there that my soul can manage is as the dark night compared with the light of the sun, or as different as is the moonlight from the sun's globe" (Prayer 19, *Prayers*, 204).

sea of sorrow."[90] And, as if this was not enough, Catherine now found herself plagued by grotesque and unrelenting temptations from the Evil One, "the demon pack with their words and acts of obscenity and lust, buzzing thick about her like a cloud of flies."[91]

In time Catherine came to understand that there was a reason why, as she puts it, "God sometimes permits her spirit to be dark and sterile and swamped by all sorts of perverse imaginings, till it seems impossible to think about God—till she can scarcely remember God's name."[92] The reason, she discovered, had to do first and last with self-knowledge:

> God permits all these struggles and this barrenness of spirit so that she will come to know herself and see that she is not. . . . Knowing herself, then, she humbles herself in her non-being and recognizes the goodness of God who through grace has given her being and every grace that is built upon being.[93]

The "night" of apparent absence of God—terrible though it is—becomes in the end the saving night of self-knowledge. And not only that; against all expectation, God, her beloved Spouse

---

90. *Dialogue*, no. 197, 99.

91. *Dialogue*, no. 108, 100–101.

92. Letter to Suor Bartolomea della Seta, T 221, *Letters*, 2:180. For some people on the path to perfection, the spiritual experience alternates between a sense of presence and a sense of absence. But for those who reach perfection, God tells Catherine: "I relieve them of this lover's game of going and coming back. I call it a 'lover's game' because I go away for love and I come back for love—no, not really I, for I am your unchanging and unchangeable God; what goes and comes back is the feeling my charity creates in the soul" (*Dialogue*, no. 78, 147).

93. *Dialogue*, no. 78, 181. St John of the Cross is at one with Catherine in emphasizing that the most immediate fruit of the dark night is growth in self-knowledge. He writes: "The first and chief benefit that this dry and dark night of contemplation causes is the knowledge of self. . . . The soul considers itself to be nothing and finds no satisfaction in self because it is aware that of itself it neither does can do anything." (*The Dark Night* 12.2, in *The Collected Works of St. John of the Cross*, trans. Kieran Kavanaugh and Otilio Rodriguez [Washington, DC: ICS, 1964], 321.

and Lord, is now found and experienced at the very heart of darkness.[94] "So," the Father says to Catherine, "I am telling you not to let these struggles distress you unduly. No, I want you to glean the light of self-knowledge from this darkness, and in that knowledge learn the virtue of humility. Be exultantly happy, realizing that at times like this I am living within you in a hidden way."[95]

vii. The Well

In a letter to Frate Tommaseo dalla Fonte, Catherine likens the inner core of the self to a well of deep, clear water. In order for us to attain to that depth—that wondrous source—we must first of all confront and acknowledge the earth, the muddied soil of our human misery. Catherine writes:

> As we discover the earth we get to the living water, the very core of the knowledge of God's true and gentle will which desires nothing else but that we be made holy. So let us enter into the depths of this well. For if we dwell there, we will necessarily come to know both ourselves and God's goodness. In recognizing that we are nothing we humble ourselves. And in humbling ourselves we enter that flaming, consumed heart, opened up like a window without shutters, never to be closed.[96]

viii. The Full Circle

In the *Dialogue*, God the Father says to Catherine: "This knowledge of yourself, and of me within yourself, is grounded in the soil

---

94. See Letter to the Monks of the Monastery of San Girolamo at Cervaia, *Letters*, 2:136.
95. Letter to Suor Bartolomea della Seta, T 221, *Letters*, 2:182.
96. Letter to Frate Tommaso dalla Fonte, T 41, *Letters*, 1:8.

of true humility."[97] It is a union, he explains, that forms a "circle" that should never be broken:

> Imagine a circle traced on the ground and, at the center of the circle, a tree with an off-shoot grafted into its side. The tree finds its nourishment in the earth within the expanse of the circle. But, were it ever uprooted from the earth, it would die, yielding no fruit. . . . It is necessary, therefore, that the root of this tree, that is the affection of the soul, should grow in and issue from the circle of true self-knowledge, knowledge that is joined to me, who, like the circle itself, have neither beginning nor end.[98]

Our most fundamental task, therefore, is to move from knowledge of God to knowledge of self and then back to knowledge of God. But should it happen, the Father warns, that knowledge of self becomes disconnected from knowledge of God, "there would be no full circle at all," and everything "would end in confusion."[99] In a more positive vein, however, the Father adds that this "circle," although clearly grounded in the plain earth of self-knowledge— the humble soil of truth—is of infinite expanse, and has "neither beginning nor end." Accordingly, by surrendering ourselves to the movement of the circle, we are able to flourish greatly, and grow like trees "made for love and living only by love."[100]

This image of the self as a tree of love recurs in one of Catherine's letters. "We are a tree of love," she writes, "because we are made for love."[101] On this occasion, however, Catherine introduces the additional theme of freedom and free choice. She writes: "This tree is so well made that no one can keep it from

---

97. *Dialogue*, no. 10, 41–42.
98. *S. Caterina da Siena: Il Dialogo*, X, ed. G. Cavallini (Rome: Edizioni Cateriniane, 1968), 24.
99. *Dialogue*, no. 10, 42.
100. *Dialogue*, no. 10, 41.
101. Letter to Countess Bandeçça Salimbeni, T 113, *Letters*, 2:677.

growing or take its fruit without the tree's consent. And God has given this tree a worker to tend it as it pleases, and this worker is free choice."[102] What matters, then, is that "free choice plants the tree where it ought to be planted, that is, in the soil of true humility."[103] And the place where this soil can be found, she goes on to say, is "the enclosed garden of self-knowledge."[104]

ix. The House

For Catherine of Siena, self-knowledge is the hinge that swings open the door of freedom, allowing us to pass from the bondage of fear and sin into the new life. "Note," she writes, "what Peter and the other disciples did that enabled them to let go of their selfish fear . . . and receive the Holy Spirit. . . . Scripture says that they shut themselves up at home and stayed there in watching and continual prayer."[105] Making clear her conviction that the witness and example of the first disciples—their devoted practice of prayer within "the house of self-knowledge"—is now the task of all believers, Catherine then adds:

> The lesson we and everyone else ought to learn from this is that we [too] must shut ourselves up at home in watching and prayer. . . . Just as Peter and the others shut themselves up at home, so those who have come to love their Father and are [God's] sons and daughters have done and ought to do. Those who want progress in

---

102. Letter to Countess Bandeçça Salimbeni, T 113, *Letters*, 2:677.
103. *Letters*, 2:677–678.
104. *Letters*, 2:678. Elsewhere Catherine writes: "First Truth has made our reason, together with our freedom of choice, to be our gardener. It is the task of reason and free choice, with the help of divine grace, to root out the brambles of vice and plant the fragrant herbs of virtue" (Letter to Abbot Martino of Passignano, T 22, *Letters*, 2:692).
105. Letter to Frate Matteo di Francisco Tolomei, T 94, *Letters*, 2:671.

this state [of perfection] must enter and shut themselves up in the house of self-knowledge.[106]

This letter was written to a young Dominican, Frate Matteo, whom Catherine had earlier helped to convert. In a separate letter, this time to Pope Urban VI, Catherine evokes once again the example of the first disciples at Pentecost, laying particular stress on the necessity of remaining within "the house of self-knowledge": "I trust that this sweet fire of the Holy Spirit will work in your heart and soul as it did in those holy disciples. . . . It seems they are teaching us how we can receive the Holy Spirit. How? We must dwell in the house of self-knowledge."[107]

In the understanding of Catherine, the illumination we receive from God in genuine self-knowledge is so strong that its radiance can in time overcome darkness; it can liberate us from the thrall of evil and from the bondage of selfish love. It should come as no surprise, therefore, to find that Catherine, when she speaks about light and the attainment of freedom, speaks also—in the same breath, as it were—about the need to remain within the house of self-knowledge:

> I long to see you in true and perfect light, the light that frees from darkness and guides us along the way of truth. . . . This is God's truth, that he created us in his image and likeness in order to give us eternal life and so that we in return might give glory

---

106. Letter to Frate Matteo di Francisco Tolomei, T 94, *Letters*, 2:671–672. "Oh how delightful to the soul and pleasing to me," the Father exclaims in the *Dialogue*, "is holy prayer made in the house of self-knowledge" (*Dialogue*, no. 66, 123).

107. Letter to Pope Urban VI, T 351, *Letters*, 4:204–205. In another place Catherine employs once again the image of fire when speaking of self-knowledge in God. It is a fire, she writes, "that burns and consumes whatever might be opposed to reason in this house. . . . Freely, freely you let yourself be guided by God's gracious will" (Letter to Frate Francisco Tebaldi of Florence, T 154, *Letters*, 4:49).

and praise to his name. . . . So it is good to seek this true and perfect light, and to use hatred to free ourselves of what deprives us of it—free ourselves, that is, from selfish love for ourselves. We will achieve this sort of hatred when we live shut up in the house of self-knowledge. There we will discover the indescribable love God has for us, and with that love we will drive out selfish love for ourselves. For a soul who sees that she is loved cannot help loving.[108]

The meaning of making use of hatred in order "to free ourselves" is further clarified in a letter that Catherine wrote to her friend Neri dei Pagliaresi: "Without that light," she notes, "everything would be done in the dark. But you cannot have this light perfectly unless you use hatred to rid yourself of the cloud of self-centeredness. Try earnestly, then, to let go of yourself so that you may gain the light."[109]

When, in the *Dialogue*, reference is made by the divine Father to "the house of self-knowledge" and to the experience of the first disciples, it is emphasized that, as soon as they received the fire of the Spirit and the grace of self-knowledge, they did not remain any longer shut up out of fear inside a *physical* house or home. On the contrary, the Father declares: "They left the house and fearlessly proclaimed my message. . . . They had no fear of suffering. . . . It did not worry them to go before the tyrants of the world to proclaim the truth."[110]

What is being enacted here is a dynamic movement from profound self-knowledge in God to the grace and energy of a

---

108. Letter to Suor Bartolomea della Seta, T 188, *Letters*, 3:194–195.
109. Letter to Neri dei Pagliaresi, T 42, *Letters*, 3:266.
110. *Dialogue*, no. 74, 136.

new self-forgetfulness, a new focus on the needs of others. "So it is with the soul," the Father says, "who has waited for me in self-knowledge. I come back to her with the fire of my charity."[111] And it is this divine fire that makes the individual soul "strong to endure suffering and to leave her house in my name to give birth to the virtues for her neighbors."[112] She does not abandon self-knowledge itself, the Father explains, because this new "impulse of love" comes forth precisely "from that house," from that source.[113] So the soul, as soon as she has attained within the house of self-knowledge to what the Father calls "perfect, free love," far from ending up in some form of cold and unhappy introversion, is in fact more truly alive than ever before, on fire with a newfound freedom: "She lets go of herself and comes out [into the open]."[114]

7. The Fire of Union with God

For St. Catherine, there is no clear path from bondage to freedom—and so no path to union with God—that does not include self-knowledge and the contemplation of the goodness of God. When, on occasion, Catherine attempts to describe that union, the image on which she relies most often is the image of fire. She writes: "I want you to live always in this knowledge of yourself, and to recognize within yourself the extravagant fire of God's charity."[115] It is there—in that "immeasurable, indescribable, incomprehensible fire"—that "the dampness of selfish love" will be dried up once and for all.[116] In a similar vein, she writes elsewhere:

---

111. *Dialogue*, no. 74, 136.
112. *Dialogue*, no. 74, 136.
113. *Dialogue*, no. 74, 137.
114. *Dialogue*, no. 74, 137.
115. Letter to Frate Francesco Tebaldi, T 154, *Letters*, 4:53.
116. *Letters*, 4:49.

I'm sure that if you are bound and set ablaze in the gentle Jesus, all the devils of hell with all their cunning will never be able to tear you away from so sweet a union. So, since this bonding is so strong and so necessary for you, I don't want you ever to stop throwing wood on the fire of holy desire—I mean the wood of self-knowledge. This is the wood that feeds the fire of divine charity, the charity that is gained by knowing God's boundless charity.[117]

Catherine, all through her life, felt the need to return to this theme of self-knowledge. It was an abiding obsession. The repeated and urgent appeal she made to her contemporaries—though now centuries old—still seems today to burn the page: "Let's not put off any longer our move into this holy dwelling of self-knowledge. We so need this, and it is so pleasant for us—because God's boundless infinite goodness is there."[118]

---

117. Letter to Raymond of Capua, T 219, *Letters*, 2:90–91. On the subject of self-knowledge and the Evil One, there is a remarkable passage in the *Dialogue* in which the Father says that the quality of Catherine's "humility of spirit" is so profound it frustrates all the attacks of the devil against her. "Damnable woman!" the devil exclaims, "There is no getting at you! If I throw you to the ground in confusion you lift yourself up to mercy. If I exalt you you throw yourself down. You come even to hell in your humility, and even in hell you hound me. So I will not come back to you again, because you beat me with the cudgel of charity!" (*Dialogue*, no. 66, 125).

118. Letter to Don Giovanni dei Sabbatini of Bologna, T 141, *Letters*, 1:145–146.

CHAPTER 5
The Shadow and the Self:
The Visions of Catherine and Jung

The phrase "Don't be afraid of your own shadow"[1] occurs in one of Catherine of Siena's letters, and it is an image that occurs many times in her writings. That same phrase, or a form of it, occurs also in the work of the modern depth psychologist Carl Gustav Jung. In his book *Aion: Researches into the Phenomenology of the Self,* while noting that a lot more people than one would expect are "afraid of the unconscious," Jung writes: "They are even afraid of their own shadow."[2] For Jung the phrase "afraid of their own shadow" carries much more weight than that of a mere colloquial or spontaneous expression. In fact, the notion of "the shadow" is of such fundamental importance in Jungian psychology that it has come to be linked with Jung more than with any other author, ancient or modern.

Needless to say, the "shadow" of which Jung speaks in his work is not the physical shadow of the body, but rather what he calls *the psychological shadow*: "that hidden, repressed, for the most part inferior and guilt-laden personality whose ultimate ramifications reach back into the realm of our animal ancestors."[3] Becoming conscious of this shadow within ourselves clearly demands a considerable moral and spiritual effort, for it is not easy

---

1. Letter to Matteo di Fazzio dei Cenni, T 124, *Letters*, 2:698.
2. Carl Gustav Jung, *Collected Works of C.G. Jung*, vol. 9, part 2, *Aion: Researches into the Phenomenology of the Self*, trans. R.F.C. Hull (Princeton, NJ: Princeton University Press, 1968), 33.
3. Jung, *Aion*, 266.

to acknowledge, as present and real, these darker, murkier aspects of our lives. Yet, Jung writes, "this act is the essential condition for any kind of self-knowledge."[4] Accordingly, however hard we may try to avoid the tough inner work of facing ourselves, such avoidance is of no avail. For in the end, as Jung tellingly points out, "nobody can dodge his own shadow."[5]

Jung would seem to be articulating here not only basic common sense but the most ancient and hallowed wisdom concerning the need for self-knowledge. For, as most readers are aware, the great religious traditions of the world, as well as the most famous schools of philosophy from ancient times, have in one form or another addressed this question. One might expect, therefore, that Jung would be content to affirm the wisdom contained in both Christian and non-Christian religious traditions. But surprisingly, with regard to Christianity, this is not the case. When Jung turns his attention to Christian tradition and reflects, in particular, on the Christian understanding of "the shadow," he is almost always negative in his assessment. Far from helping humanity in its distress, the Christian vision, according to Jung, actually deepens humanity's sense of guilt and distress. How are we to understand and respond to this challenge?

I propose, in the pages that follow, to present as clearly and accurately as possible Jung's teaching regarding "the shadow," and then allow Catherine of Siena to speak as a representative of the Christian vision. It goes without saying that, in the medieval work of Catherine, we don't find the technical scientific language and understanding that have been developed in modern depth psychology. But Jung himself would be the first to assert that what

---

4. Jung, *Aion*, 8.
5. C.G. Jung, *Collected Works of C.G. Jung*, vol. 10, *Civilization in Transition*, trans. R.F.C. Hull (Princeton, NJ: Princeton University Press, 1970), 170.

is meant in his work by "the shadow" is not some kind of strange darkness or neurosis exclusive to the modern world, but rather a dimension of human experience manifestly present in every age and in every person.

1. Jung on the Shadow

The attempt to uncover, with clarity and precision, the meaning or meanings Jung gives to the term "shadow" in his work presents a not inconsiderable challenge. Unlike his colleague Sigmund Freud, whose talent as an author (whatever we may think of his ideas) is universally acknowledged, Jung tends to be decidedly elusive in both thought and expression. That said, however, his numerous reflections on "the shadow" constitute what are undoubtedly some of the most vivid and fascinating pages in modern depth psychology.

On one subject, Catherine of Siena and Carl Gustav Jung find themselves in manifest agreement: they are both happily persuaded of the critical importance of self-knowledge, and of the need to engage, at some fundamental level, in the practice of meditation. Jung writes: "In general, meditation and contemplation have a bad reputation in the West. They are regarded as a particularly reprehensible form of idleness or as pathological narcissism. No one has time for self-knowledge."[6] The result of this negative attitude is that people find themselves bereft very often of even the most basic forms and practices of interiority. All the focus in life goes on external achievement and success—on *doing*, and not on the *doer*. "Western man confronts himself as a stranger."[7]

---

6. C.G. Jung, *Collected Works of C.G. Jung*, vol. 14, *Mysterium Coniunctionis*, trans. R.F.C. Hull (Princeton, NJ: Princeton University Press, 1970), 498.

7. Jung, *Mysterium Coniunctionis*, 498.

Once we take the risk of coming to know ourselves, one of the key discoveries we make—and it is a painful discovery—is that we are a lot "less good" than we had imagined.[8] According to Jung, it is this new, troubling awareness that marks the beginning of our confrontation with "the shadow." He writes: "It is a frightening thought that man also has a shadow side to him, consisting not just of little weaknesses and foibles, but of a positively demonic dynamism."[9] At one point, Jung goes so far as to describe the reality of the shadow as "the invisible saurian tail that man still drags behind him."[10] It is a phenomenon made up of all the real or potential negatives within ourselves; the dark side of our psyche; the unacknowledged evil "brother," if you like; the shadow-self whose presence we have never wanted to acknowledge, and whose reality we have instinctively suppressed.[11]

Allowing "the shadow" to emerge into consciousness initiates what Jung calls the individuation process. This marks a stage in personal growth when unconscious elements in the psyche, hitherto repressed, are at last made conscious. It is—Jung points out with marked insistence—a stage of growth as necessary as it is demanding:

---

8. See C.G. Jung, "Psychology and Religion," in *Collected Works of C.G. Jung*, vol. 11, *Psychology and Religion: West and East*, trans. R.F.C. Hull (Princeton, NJ: Princeton University Press, 1958), 131.

9. C.G. Jung, "On the Psychology of the Unconscious," in *Collected Works of C.G. Jung*, vol. 7, *Two Essays on Analytical Psychology* (Princeton, NJ: Princeton University Press, 1972), 35.

10. C.G. Jung, "The Integration of the Personality," in *C.G. Jung: Psychological Reflections: A New Anthology of His Works 1905-1961*, ed. J. Jacobi (Princeton, NJ: Princeton University Press, 1973), 217.

11. In other places, however, Jung declares that the shadow, while often manifesting itself as "inferior, unadapted, and awkward," is "not wholly bad." He writes: "It even contains childish or primitive qualities which would in a way vitalize and embellish human existence" (Jung, *Psychology and Religion*, 78).

In this way man becomes for himself the difficult problem he really is. He must always remain conscious of the fact that he is such a problem if he wants to develop at all. Repression leads to a one-sided development if not to stagnation, and eventually to neurotic dissociation. Today it is no longer a question of "How can I get rid of my shadow?"—for we have seen enough of the curse of one-sidedness. Rather we must ask ourselves: "How can man live with his shadow without its precipitating a succession of disasters?"[12]

Should an individual choose to ignore completely his dark or bad side—should he cling to a perception of himself as someone always "on the side of light," as someone basically good—then the repressed shadow side of his being will inevitably become, according to Jung, even more dark, even more ugly. He writes: "Everyone carries a shadow, and the less it is embodied in the individual conscious life, the blacker and denser it is. ... If it is repressed and isolated from consciousness, it never gets corrected."[13]

What we are left with, then, is what Jung calls "a man without a shadow"—an individual, in other words, "who imagines he actually *is* only what he cares to know about himself."[14] And that man can become a veritable danger both to himself and others. "It is often tragic to see," Jung observes, "how blatantly a man bungles his own life and the lives of others yet remains totally incapable of seeing how much the whole tragedy originates in himself, and

---

12. C.G. Jung, *Collected Works of C.G. Jung*, vol. 16, *The Practice of Psychotherapy*, trans. R.F.C. Hull (Princeton, NJ: Princeton University Press, 1966), 239.

13. Jung, "Psychology and Religion," in *Psychology and Religion*, 131.

14. C.G. Jung, *Collected Works of C.G. Jung*, vol. 8, *The Structure and Dynamics of the Psyche*, trans. R.F.C. Hull (Princeton, NJ: Princeton University Press, 1969), 208.

how he continually feeds it and keeps it going."[15] Such a man (and I am using the word "man" here, as Jung uses it in his work, to refer to both men and women), refusing to acknowledge the dark "inferior personality" lurking within, instinctively projects that shadow, that darkness, that cold unlovely specter, onto others, all while remaining quite unaware of what he's doing. Jung asserts: "A man who is unconscious of himself acts in a blind, instinctive way and is in addition fooled by all the illusions that arise when he sees everything that he is not conscious of in himself coming to meet him from outside as projections upon his neighbor."[16]

Jung's basic insight here corresponds to a striking degree (as will be demonstrated later) with the teaching of Catherine of Siena. And this invites speculation, because it is precisely the Christian way of responding to "the shadow" that Jung, in his work, denounces as unenlightened and dangerous. What, then, it must be asked, is the basis for Jung's opposition? In what way is his understanding of "the shadow" radically different from that of a Christian author such as Catherine of Siena? By far the best way to explore these questions, and hopefully find an answer, is to focus attention on the following two areas of vision in the work of Jung and of Catherine: their understanding of the relation of the shadow to God, and then of the shadow to the self.

2. The Shadow and God

In 1932, reflecting on the question of religion and the role religion plays in people's lives, Jung had this to say:

---

15. Jung, *Aion*, 10.
16. C.G. Jung, "The Philosophical Tree," in *Collected Works of C.G. Jung*, vol. 13, *Alchemical Studies*, trans. R.F.C. Hull (Princeton, NJ: Princeton University Press, 1967), 335.

Among all my patients in the second half of life—that is to say, over thirty five—there has not been one whose problem in the last resort was not that of finding a religious outlook on life. It is safe to say that every one of them fell ill because he has lost that which the living religions of every age have given to their followers, and none of them has been really healed who did not regain his religious outlook.[17]

Freud, one of Jung's early mentors, had been manifestly hostile to religion.[18] Not so Jung. On the strength of the passage just quoted, any religious believer might confidently conclude that Jung was a friend and advocate of religion in its most basic forms. That certainly was the impression received by the Dominican priest Victor White when he first came upon the writings of Jung. Years later, however, when White became more familiar with Jung's work (and with the man himself), he declared: "I think that the friendliness of Jung represents a far more serious and radical challenge to religion as we know it than did ever the hostility of Freud."[19]

In White's opinion, the principal danger for religious belief resided in Jung's understanding of the relationship between "the shadow" and God, an understanding that believers might be tempted to embrace without realizing the implications of their innocent enthusiasm—without recognizing, that is, how

---

17. C.G. Jung, *Modern Man in Search of a Soul*, trans. W.S. Dell and C.F. Baynes (London: Kegan Paul, Trench, Trubner and Co, 1933), 264.

18. Jung, prior to his collaboration with Freud, had other mentors. He owed, for example, a debt to French psychiatry (Pierre Janet), and to Theodore Flournoy, who had already by 1910 elaborated a conception of the creative unconscious. See Henri F. Ellenberger, *The Discovery of the Unconscious: The History and Evolution of Dynamic Psychiatry* (New York: Basic Books, 1970).

19. Victor White, "Challenges to Religion," *Commonweal* 55 (1952): 561–562.

profoundly different Jung's vision was from their own. One of the
basic tenets of Christian belief is that "God is light and in him
there is no darkness at all" (1 John 1:5). Not the least shadow of
evil, therefore, exists in the divine nature.[20] God, for Catherine of
Siena, is a God of unimaginable goodness; he is "light surpassing
all other light,"[21] and "he is supreme wisdom, supreme power,
supreme mercy, and supreme beauty—so beautiful that the sun
marvels at his beauty."[22]

Addressing the eternal Father, Catherine exclaims: "I am
darkness and you are light. I am ignorance and you are wisdom.
You are infinite and I am finite. I am sick and you are the
doctor. I am a weak sinner who has never loved you. You are
purest beauty."[23] Catherine, it should be noted, though capable
of expressing her weakness and limitation in such vivid terms,
maintains nevertheless a profound sense of her own "dignity and
beauty" in the eyes of God.[24] Made in God's image, her nature
at its core is not something to be disdained. Formed from the
very beginning in the likeness of the divine nature, it bears God's
image: it is living fire.[25]

The belief that in God there is not the least shadow of darkness,
not the least hint of evil, Jung finds impossible to accept. In his
understanding, unimaginable evil belongs to the Godhead just as
much as tremendous goodness. "God," he declares, "has a terrible

---

20. See Letter to Sano di Maco, T 62, *Letters*, 2:605: "We see that God is
supremely good, and that nothing other than supreme goodness can come from
him."

21. *Dialogue*, no. 134, 273. See also Letter T 264, *Letters*, 2:479: "He is light,
the source of our light."

22. Letter to Francesco di Tato Tolomei, T 81, *Letters*, 3:39.

23. Prayer 1, *Prayers*, 50.

24. *Dialogue*, no. 13, 48.

25. Prayer 12, *Prayers*, 117.

double aspect: a sea of grace is met with a seething lake of fire."[26] Being the Creator, the origin of all, God is the direct cause not only of the beauty we witness on earth but also of the horror. On this subject, White summarizes Jung's thinking as follows: "On the principle that things are what they do—*omne agens agit sibi simile*—God therefore is darkness as well as light, evil as well as peace."[27]

By any standard, these are startling declarations. They constitute a direct contradiction of Christian belief. But it would, I think, be amiss to conclude that they have their origin in some kind of emotional or intellectual willfulness. Jung's rejection of a central tenet of the Christian vision, however profoundly mistaken and regrettable, cannot be dismissed out of hand as a mere fit of petulance or ill temper. The most immediate context for his reflections on the subject of evil was the horror endured by countless numbers of people in Europe during the First and Second World Wars. In 1916 he spoke of "mass murder" being committed "on an unparalleled scale."[28] And in 1952, after the overwhelming event of the Shoah, he wrote: "We have experienced things so unheard-of and so staggering that the question of whether such things are in any way reconcilable with the idea of a good God has become burningly topical. It is no longer a problem for experts in theological seminaries, but a universal religious nightmare."[29]

---

26. Jung, "Answer to Job," in *Psychology and Religion*, 89. To anyone who has knowledge of ancient Gnostic mythology, this disturbing image of the Godhead will be familiar. The fact that Jung was for many years directly influenced by Gnosticism is now generally accepted by scholars. What is open to debate, and a matter of considerable controversy, is the extent of that influence. Jung himself speaks of "the astonishing parallelism between Gnostic symbolism and the findings of the psychology of the unconscious" (Jung, "The Structure and Dynamics of the Self," in *Aion*, 223).

27. Victor White, *Soul and Psyche: An Enquiry into the Relationship of Psychotherapy and Religion* (New York: Harper, 1960), 223.

28. Jung, "The Archetypes of the Collective Unconscious" in *Two Essays on Analytical Psychology*, 35.

29. Jung, "Answer to Job," in *Psychology and Religion*, 91.

Apart from this "nightmare," Jung had one other reason for thinking it necessary to place evil in the Godhead. Since God was viewed in the Christian religion as a God without shadow, everything that the shadow contained, he believed—including all the blame for the horror, and all the guilt—would inevitably fall back on human beings. "Since the reality of darkness and evil could not be denied, there was no alternative but to make man responsible for it. . . . Man, thereupon, became the real carrier of the *mysterium iniquitatis* [the mystery of iniquity]: *omne bonum a Deo, omne malum ab homine* [all good from God, all evil from man]."[30]

The assertion that God is the *summum bonum*, a God in whom there is no shadow of evil, has the effect, Jung believes, of placing an unbearable weight of guilt on the shoulders of human beings. But also, paradoxically, it can have the opposite effect: an ignoring, on the part of Christian believers, of the true horror of evil, and an attempt to regard evil as something less than truly terrifying, a harmless absence of good—a *privatio boni*. In Jung's understanding, this theological formula is not only highly suspect; it is altogether abhorrent. In a letter to White on December 31, 1949, he writes: "This *privatio boni* business is odious to me."[31] Elsewhere, he declares that the formula "robs evil of its absolute existence."[32] In effect, it trivializes sin. He writes: "As long as Evil is a non-being nobody will take his own shadow seriously. . . . This goes to the very roots of Christianity. Evil does not decrease by

30. Jung, "Psychological Aspects of the Mother Archetype," in *Collected Works of C.G. Jung*, vol. 9, part 1, *The Archetypes and the Collective Unconscious*, trans. R.F.C. Hull (Princeton, NJ: Princeton University Press, 1981), 103.

31. *Letters of Carl Gustav Jung: 1906-1950*, vol. 1, ed. Gerhard Adler (Princeton, NJ: Princeton University Press, 1973), 541.

32. A phrase from Jung's Eranos lecture (1940), cited by Ann Conrad Lammers, *In God's Shadow: The Collaboration of C.G. Jung and Victor White* (New York: Paulist, 1994), 172.

being hushed up as a non-reality or as mere negligence of man."³³

Victor White, in his response to this vehement attack, states simply and clearly that Jung has a mistaken understanding of *privatio boni*. He writes: "This idea that evil is 'nothing,' 'a trifling diminution of good,' is a grotesque caricature of anything that has ever been generally held in the Catholic Church."³⁴ Evil people and evil things, evil deeds and inclinations, are "very real and very powerful," he says. So real, in fact, that "it is at our peril that we pretend to ourselves that they are not."³⁵ The teaching on evil, indicated by the phrase *privatio boni*, has found expression over the centuries not only in much Christian reflection but also in the writings of some of the finest Greek philosophers. And clear echoes of that teaching can also be found, as it happens, in the writings of Catherine of Siena.

The spring of 1374 marks the first time this teaching, or an echo of it, appears in Catherine's work. She writes: "That which has no being—sin, I mean—is not in God."³⁶ This notion of the "nothingness" of sin we find repeated by Catherine in a particularly striking way toward the end of January 1377: "We cannot bring a greater wretchedness on ourselves than to become the servants and slaves of sin, since we thereby lose the being that is grace. We serve nothingness and we become nothings."³⁷ Although the naming of sin as a form of *nonbeing* may well sound strange at first hearing, it's clear from what Catherine is saying here that in no way does she regard sin or evil as something relatively minor,

---

33. Jung to White, December 21, 1949, *Letters of C.G. Jung*, 1:8.
34. White, *Soul and Psyche*, 154.
35. White, *Soul and Psyche*, 152.
36. Letter to the Abbess and Suora Niccolosa, T 30, *Letters*, 1:49–50.
37. Letter to Pietro di Missere, T 254, *Letters*, 2:294–295.

"a mere . . . cloud passing over the sun."[38] On the contrary, for Catherine, it is impossible to imagine "a greater wretchedness."

In her work, Catherine never quotes the Latin formula *privatio boni*, but the ideas associated with it are everywhere present in her writings. When God the Father speaks to her in the *Dialogue* concerning the question of sin, the language in which he speaks appears to echo that of Aquinas and the scholastics: "I am the Creator of everything that has any share in being. But sin is not of my making, for sin is non-being."[39] At the level of metaphysics, the point could hardly be made more clearly. In God there is not the least shadow of evil or sin. Everything God creates must be good. But if this is indeed the case, are we to conclude then that the shadow belongs, first and last, to human beings? In light of St. Catherine's teaching, how are we to understand—how are we to *transform*—what Jung calls "the abysmal darkness of human nature"?[40]

3. The Shadow and the Self

"Everyone carries a shadow, and the less it is embodied in the individual's conscious life, the blacker and denser it is."[41] Fired by this conviction, Jung regards as imperative the *conscious* acknowledgment of the shadow by each individual, a task of mind and heart that begins the long, necessary process of integrating the shadow. But the process, he argues, has not been aided by Christianity. In particular, medieval Catholicism has shown itself incapable of dealing with evil effectively. According to Jung, it

---

38. A phrase of Jung's cited by White in *Soul and Psyche*, 154.
39. *Dialogue*, no. 18, 56.
40. Jung, "The Spirit Mercurius," in *Alchemical Studies*, 244.
41. Jung, "Psychology and Religion," in *Psychology and Religion*, 76.

failed humanity "four hundred years ago," and the mentality it enshrines is, at the present time, "more of a failure than ever, and in the most terrible way."[42]

Jung believes that the medieval mentality, instead of marking out the path that leads to authentic self-knowledge, and thus to an awareness of the shadow lurking within, does the very opposite. It encourages each individual to live, from one day to the next, a naive and primitive existence—psychologically speaking—unaware of the truly dark and dangerous side of human nature.[43] That such an unhappy split exists between the ego and the shadow in countless numbers of people and in every generation is unquestionably the case. But to claim that this division within the self is something almost uniquely characteristic of medieval Catholicism will puzzle anyone familiar with the life and literature of the Middle Ages.

There are innumerable tracts, treatises, sermons, paintings, and poems from the Middle Ages that highlight the dark side of human nature, the sad human tendency to commit and be complicit with evil. It's astonishing therefore to hear the Middle Ages—of all periods—being accused of not taking evil seriously. The sharp, unmistakable irony of the attack was not lost on White. He remarked: "The view that Christianity encourages a smug optimism which represses evil and the dark side of life may be a welcome change from the more usual charge that it is forever harping on suffering and sin, the corruption of our fallen nature, on hell-fire and the necessity for carrying our cross."[44]

---

42. Jung to Irminger, September 22, 1944, *Letters of C.G. Jung*, 1:349. The letter was never sent, but Jung kept it in his library.

43. According to Jung, one of the reasons for Christianity's failure to deal accurately with "the shadow" was "Christian abhorrence of anything Gnostic" (Jung, "Psychology and Religion," in *Psychology and Religion*, 77).

44. White, *Soul and Psyche*, 151.

In the English medieval text *The Scale of Perfection*, the author Walter Hilton (an almost exact contemporary of Catherine of Siena) speaks with unusual clarity about the encounter with "the shadow," an encounter that, he explains, takes place at a certain stage in meditation. For Hilton the shadow is a "murk image" of the self—quite a startling revelation, therefore, and yet an experience familiar over the centuries in the lives of other Christian believers and contemplatives. St. Paul, he writes, "bore this image often very heavy."[45]

The individual contemplative, expecting to encounter in meditation nothing except the living presence of Christ Jesus, is initially shocked at coming face to face *not* with the radiant Lord of his desire but rather with the stark fact of his own inner darkness. It is, Hilton writes, a moment for honest self-assessment and purification. In this "spiritual darkness," he writes, "you need to toil [literally *swink*] and sweat."[46] Hilton is fully aware that without at some point encountering the reality of the shadow, there can be no possible union with God. And this, he admits, will be painful:

> For vain thoughts are always wanting to press thickly into your heart, to draw your thought down to them; but you shall withstand them; and if you do so you shall find something—though not Jesus whom you seek. What, then? Indeed nothing but a dark and painful image of your own soul, which has neither the light of knowledge nor the feeling of love or pleasure. If you look at it plainly, this image is all wrapped up in black stinking clothes of sin, such as pride, envy, wrath, *accidie*, covetousness, gluttony and

---

45. Walter Hilton, *The Scale of Perfection*, trans. John P.H. Clark and Rosemary Dorward (New York: Paulist Press, 1991), 125.
46. Hilton, *The Scale of Perfection*, 125.

lechery. . . . This image and this black shadow you carry about with you wherever you go.[47]

Catherine of Siena, in attempting to describe the phenomenon of the "black shadow" and the acceptance of it, employs a number of different phrases such as "the dark of self-knowledge" (*la tenebra del cognoscimento di se*).[48] The phrase is both memorable and significant. In the text where it occurs, Catherine notes, as if by way of explanation: "If we do not see our own darkness we cannot know the love and light of divine goodness."[49] In the *Dialogue*, reference is made at one point to the dark blemish (*la macula*) that we see on the face of our soul when we approach the mirror of God's truth—in Catherine's phrase, "la macula della faccia dell'uomo" (the dark blemish of the human face).[50] Though it is manifestly painful for human beings to accept, "the dark of self-knowledge" is knowledge that must somehow be acquired. Nevertheless, "it would not be good," Catherine warns, "to dwell exclusively in this knowledge of ourselves because we would become discouraged and weary, and from discouragement we would end up in despair."[51]

---

47. Hilton, *The Scale of Perfection*, 124. In a parallel passage, George Fox, the founder of the Society of Friends, speaks in his journal of a particular phase in meditation when things that he had considered dark and evil in the world *outside* himself, he finds to his astonishment to be also *within*. There was "an ocean of darkness," he writes, but also "an ocean of light and love which flowed over the ocean of darkness. In that also I saw the infinite love of God, and I had great openings." Commenting on this Journal entry, P.W. Martin remarks: "It is in facing and dealing with the shadow, the dark gateway to the deep unconscious, that a man realizes himself for the first time; and with this realization may find a sense of community with others and come upon the 'great openings' of the spirit." (Martin, *Experiment in Depth: A Study of the Work of Jung, Eliot and Toynbee* [London: Routledge & Kegan Paul, 1955], 78).

48. Letter to the Prior and Brothers of the Company of the Virgin Mary, T 184, *Letters*, 2:311. For the original Italian text, see *Le Lettere*, 3:117.

49. *Letters*, 2:311.

50. *Dialogue*, no. 13, 48.

51. Letter to Nanna, daughter of Catherine's eldest brother, T 23, *Letters*, 2:558.

When Catherine exhorts, in one form or another, "Don't be afraid of your own shadow," what she has in mind most often is the issue of cowardice and timidity—the fear we have of confronting suffering. But when, in one particular letter to a young Benedictine monk, she declares, "We mustn't be afraid," her most immediate concern is the monk's fear of his own inner darkness.[52] On this occasion, what she recommends is a practice not dissimilar to modern psychological theory: the hidden and repressed fears and thoughts, however murky, should be brought out into the light and shared with another individual. Here, the trusted listener Catherine has in mind is not, needless to say, a psychologist, but rather a wise spiritual guide or confessor: "When [evil] thoughts or strong temptations regarding some specific thing (no matter how ugly) come into your heart, never keep them inside, but reveal them to the father of your soul. . . . We mustn't be afraid, but must reveal our every infirmity to the doctor of our soul."[53]

4. The Shadow of Guilt and Projection

No aspect of Jung's teaching on "the shadow" is more worthy of study than his reflections on the phenomenon that he calls "projection." The word itself, of course, is never employed by Catherine of Siena. Nevertheless, a number of her reflections on the subject, and Jung's own reflections, are thrown helpfully into relief as soon as the two visions are placed alongside one another.

The shadow aspect of our nature, which needs to be acknowledged with humility and courage, is, according to Jung, "that dark half of the psyche which we invariably get rid of by means of projection."[54] That means, in practice, "burdening

---

52. Letter to Niccolò di Nanni, T 287b, *Letters*, 2:651.
53. *Letters*, 2:650–651.
54. Jung, "Introduction to the Religious and Psychological Problems of Alchemy," in *Collected Works of C.G. Jung*, vol. 12, *Psychology and Alchemy*, trans. R.F.C. Hull (Princeton, NJ: Princeton University Press, 1980), 29.

our neighbors . . . with all the faults which we obviously have ourselves."[55] Jung points out that "if the individual is to take stock of himself it is essential that his projections should be recognized,"[56] for two reasons: first of all, because the face of the neighbor has been falsified by the projection, and second, because the things that have been projected belong to one's own personality and need to be integrated with it. "This," Jung remarks, "is one of the most important phases in the wearisome process of self-knowledge."[57]

For an individual to own up to the fact that he has been avoiding his own shadow by falsely projecting it onto others is "a moral achievement beyond the ordinary."[58] Normally, the individual will be inclined to persist in his mistaken idea that the real problem lies with the *other person*:

> No matter how obvious it may be to the neutral observer that it is a matter of projections, there is little hope that the subject will perceive this himself. He must be convinced that he throws a very long shadow before he is willing to withdraw his emotionally-toned projections from their object.[59]

Unless the individual has the courage and insight to make that change, he remains effectively blind to what is happening all around him. "How can anyone see straight when he does not even see himself and the darkness he unconsciously carries with him into all his dealings?"[60]

The accuracy of Jung's insights on this particular subject is unmatched by any author of the twentieth century with whose

55. Jung, *Psychology and Alchemy*, 29.
56. Jung, *Mysterium Coniunctionis*, 499.
57. Jung, *Mysterium Coniunctionis*, 499.
58. Jung, *Aion*, 9.
59. Jung, *Aion*, 9.
60. Jung, *Psychology and Religion*, 83.

work I am familiar. Jung himself, to my knowledge, had never read any of the work of Catherine of Siena. And perhaps this is not surprising. His view of medieval Christianity was almost entirely negative, regarding it for the most part as a religion both primitive and dangerously naive.[61] But if the Swiss doctor had found time to read even a little of the work of Catherine, he would, I suspect, have been struck by the range and depth of her teaching on the need for self-knowledge. And he would also, most likely, have been astonished to find more than a few traces of his own wise teaching on projection.

It is of critical importance, for both Catherine and Jung, that the darkness we project onto others be acknowledged openly and honestly as our own darkness. In one of her letters speaking of how, by living an escapist and superficial life, the individual can become "afraid of his own shadow," Catherine notes that it is possible for that same person to become even "more afraid of the shadow of another"—but that shadow, she declares, is "really his own shadow" (*l'ombra sua*).[62] The solution for Catherine is self-knowledge in God: "I beg you—I beg you and myself and every servant of God—let's concentrate on getting to know ourselves perfectly, so that we may more perfectly know God's goodness. Then, with the light, let's give up judging our neighbors, and take up genuine compassion."[63]

Without at least some acknowledgment of the shadow, both authors agree, there can be no attainment to light, and no

---

61. But on occasion Jung was willing to acknowledge the lasting (positive) influence on our world of "the Christian Middle Ages": "Everything we think is the fruit of the Middle Ages. . . . Our whole science, everything that passes through our head, has inevitably gone through this history" (Seminar at Basel, October 1934, cited in White, *Soul and Psyche*, 67).
62. Letter to Bishop Angelo Ricasoli, T 88, *Le Lettere*, 2:77 (emphasis added).
63. Letter to Daniella of Orvieto, T 65, *Letters*, 3:239.

growth in human kindness and compassion either. Both Jung and Catherine are concerned to liberate their contemporaries from certain ingrained habits of projection. For without what Jung calls "the individuation process"—the painful acknowledgement of one's own dark shadow—there can be no escape from the dual bondage of repression and projection.

5. Saints and the Shadow

In the life of St. Paul, "the shadow" found its most vivid expression in the profound humiliation he endured because of "the thorn in his flesh." Paul writes in 2 Corinthians 12:7, "To keep me from being too elated [by the abundance of revelations], a thorn was given me in the flesh, a messenger of Satan to torment me."[64] Three times he begged the Lord to be freed from it, but without success. The "thorn"—referred to in Catherine's *Dialogue* as "the pricking and resistance of his flesh"[65]—remained. But in the *Dialogue*, addressing directly this particular dilemma of St. Paul, we hear the following response from the divine Father:

> Could I and can I not make it otherwise for Paul and the others in whom I leave this or that sort of pricking? Yes. Then why does my providence do this? To give them opportunity for merit, to keep them in the self-knowledge whence they draw true humility, to make them compassionate instead of cruel toward their neighbors so that they will sympathize with them in their labors. For those who suffer themselves are far more compassionate to the suffering than are those who have not suffered.[66]

---

64. Worth placing beside this text is St. Paul's declaration in Romans 7:15–16: "I do not understand my own actions. For I do not do what I want, but I do the very thing I hate. Now if I do what I do not want, I agree that the law is good."

65. *Dialogue*, no. 145, 305.

66. *Dialogue*, no. 145, 305.

Men and women who have never been deeply afflicted in life, and who imagine they have no shadow, often feel they have the right to judge the intimate lives of others. "They have no perception yet of themselves," Catherine writes, "and still they want to investigate the affairs of others under the pretext of doing good."[67] Hugh of St. Victor, a medieval author of the twelfth century, calls this tendency "the vice of curious inquiry."[68] Anyone who lives day to day completely unaware of his or her own weakness is a person incapable of human tact or kindness: "The less he thinks within himself that merits blame, the readier he is to hunt down someone else."[69]

Another medieval author and a near contemporary of Catherine, the Dominican preacher Johannes Tauler, speaks of "the unspeakable harmful tendency" of passing judgment on others:

> This tendency is deeply rooted in human nature and many people are guilty of it. It is an evil inclination that makes a man willing to always judge others without ever attempting to judge himself. ... Thus one inflicts on one's neighbor the same wound which one bears oneself, by passing the evil judgment on to him.[70]

Catherine repeats statements of this kind over and over again: "Don't waste time in idle talk or in meddling in the affairs of others, feeding on your neighbors' flesh in grumbling and rash judgment (for God alone is supreme Judge over us and everyone)."[71] On the question of judgment, however, there was one thing that greatly puzzled Catherine. From an early age, she had received the gift

---

67. Letter to Matteo di Tomuccio of Orvieto, T 197, *Letters*, 2:429.
68. Hugh of St. Victor, "Noah's Ark," in *Selected Spiritual Writings*, trans. a religious of CSMV (London: Faber, 1962), 109.
69. Hugh, *Selected Spiritual Writings*, 109.
70. Sermon 27, in *Johannes Tauler: Sermons* (New York: Paulist, 1985), 100.
71. Letter to Sano di Maco, T 318, Letters, 4:109.

of "reading souls." Sometimes, when at prayer, she would see one individual in light, and another in darkness. Did this not mean that she was, in some sense, sharing in God's judgment?

The answer Catherine receives from the eternal Father in the *Dialogue* is sharp and clear: "Leave this and every other kind of judgment to me, because it is my prerogative, not yours. Give up judgment, which belongs to me, and take up compassion."[72] Even if Catherine should happen to observe in a particular individual "a confused and darksome spirit," she should not assume that "the person is guilty of serious sin."[73] Often as not, the Father tells her, her judgment would be false. The "darkness" that she perceives could indeed, it's true, be an indication of sinfulness, but it could also be a sign of a mysterious grace (that phenomenon later mystics would call "the dark night") that God is working in the soul. And knowledge of the difference between the two kinds of darkness is available only to God.[74] Catherine's task, therefore, in spite of her many extraordinary gifts, was to pray, not to judge. "Compassion," the Father tells her, "is what you must have, you and the others, and leave the judging to me."[75]

One of the most striking moments in the *Dialogue* occurs when Catherine openly confesses that she had been guilty of judging other people. Of this sin, however, this "sickness," she was completely unaware until God intervened to give her a much-needed dose of self-knowledge:

> You gave me as well a medicine against a hidden sickness I had not recognized, by teaching me that I can never sit in judgment on any person, especially on your servants. For I, blind and weak as I was

---

72. *Dialogue*, no. 103, 195.
73. *Dialogue*, no. 103, 194.
74. *Dialogue*, no. 103, 195.
75. *Dialogue*, no. 105, 197.

from this sickness, have often judged others under the pretext of
working for your honor and their salvation. So I thank you, high
eternal Goodness, for . . . making me aware of my weakness. I ask
you, therefore, for grace and mercy, that today I may make an end
once and for all of straying from the teaching you have given me
and to whoever is willing to follow it.[76]

This Gospel teaching Catherine passes on to all those with
whom she is in contact, and at every opportunity. Instead of
constantly focusing attention on the weaknesses of others, she
urges them to adopt a totally different approach: "Realize that
we shouldn't trust everything we see, but should put it behind
our back, so that we will simply be left looking at and knowing
ourselves."[77] All men and women have within themselves difficult
things they need to face—that goes without saying. But rather than
confront them, our human tendency, Catherine says, is "to unload
these burdens onto others."[78] Blame takes the place of shame, and
the shadow of real or possible guilt is attributed to other people.
But this, she insists, we must not do: "No, we must attribute it to
ourselves and our own sins, each one of us."[79]

In making this statement and others like it, Catherine does
not mean that we should close our eyes to the evil taking place
around us. On the contrary, like Jung facing the horrors of the
twentieth century, she knew, as she confronted the tragedies
of her own age, "the evil which comes to light in man and that
undoubtedly dwells within him is of gigantic proportions."[80] In

76. *Dialogue*, no. 108, 202.
77. Letter to Daniella of Orvieto, T 65, *Letters*, 3:238.
78. Letter to a Woman in Florence, T 307, *Letters*, 3:322.
79. *Letters*, 3:322.
80. Jung, "The Undiscovered Self," in *Civilization in Transition*, 296.

one of the most insightful and courageous passages in his work, Jung writes:

> The evil, the guilt, the profound unease of conscience, the dark foreboding, are there before our eyes, if only we would see. Man has done these things; I am a man, who has his share of human nature; therefore I am guilty with the rest and bear unaltered and indelibly within me the capacity and the inclination to do them again at any time. Even if, juristically speaking, we were not accessories to the crime, we are always, thanks to our human nature, potential criminals. . . . None of us stands outside humanity's black collective shadow.[81]

Over time Catherine came to understand that she had no right simply to condemn evil from the outside without first admitting her own complicity with evil. This is why she would instinctively offer advice such as the following: "The vice you thought you were recognizing in others, put it on your own back."[82] It's also why she did not hesitate to make the following direct appeal to some of the women closest to her in Siena: "Be compassionate about my sins, which are the cause of the evils committed throughout the world."[83] Catherine, we know, was forever exhorting others not to be afraid of their own shadow, and yet, on at least one occasion, we hear her exclaim: "My own shadow has made me afraid" (*L'ombra mia mi ha fatto paura*).[84] Fear, in Catherine's understanding, was almost always regarded as having a destructive potential, and yet she admitted to her spiritual director: "I confess and do not deny that this root has not been weeded out of my soul."[85]

---

81. Jung, "The Undiscovered Self," in *Civilization in Transition*, 296–297.
82. Letter to Daniella of Orvieto, T 65, *Letters*, 3:238.
83. Letter to Monna Alessa dei Saracini, T 286, *Letters*, 3:54.
84. Letter to Pietro Canigiani, T 96, *Le Lettere*, 2:107.
85. Letter to Raymond, T 344, *Letters*, 4:229.

❁

My aim in this chapter has been to explore one particular theme in the work of Jung and Catherine—an ambitious aim, obviously, because one brief chapter cannot hope to do justice to the work of either Jung or Catherine. Nevertheless, if I'm not mistaken, one thing has emerged clearly from our study. In spite of the manifest differences between their two visions—one medieval, one modern—when it comes to the subject of "the shadow," it is undeniable that there are also points of surprising and important agreement in their work.

For both Jung and Catherine this particular subject was obviously never one of mere academic interest. Both lived through periods in human history of unique horror. And so the question of what Jung called "the shadow," the question of the reality of evil in the world and of the horror of human involvement in evil, was front and center. Concerned that human beings should not have to bear the full weight of responsibility for evil, Jung chose to place evil in God, or in the God-image, a decision based largely, it would seem, on the influence of the Gnostic tradition.[86] Needless to say, for the majority of Christian believers and thinkers, this was a truly appalling decision.

Whether Jung's intention was to speak of the God of history—the actual, living God—or merely of the God of myth (a question still much debated by Jungians and others[87]), the

---

86. On the question of Jung's relation to Gnosticism, see footnote 26 on page 111 above.

87. The question has been explored mainly with reference to two different kinds of understanding: that of metaphysics and that of psychology. Jung often claimed that he was writing not as a philosopher or a theologian but merely as an empirical observer. But on this question John P. Dourley writes: "In so far as metaphysics can be understood as dealing with what is and how it is known, [Jung's] psychology does indeed include a latent metaphysic, and Jung should have shown more candor in admitting it" ("In the Shadow of the Monotheisms: Jung's Conversations with Buber and White," in *Jung and the Monotheisms: Judaism, Christianity and Islam*, ed. J. Ryce-Menuhin [New York: Routledge, 1994], 133). See also Lammers, *In God's Shadow*, 129, 169, 180–182, 189, 231.

placing of evil in the Godhead marked a decisive break with mainstream Christian tradition. Jung, quite early on in his career, became convinced that the age-old Christian insistence on the absolute goodness of God left believers in an unhappy and dangerous dilemma. Not having a model in the Godhead that would help them to integrate the darker dimensions of their own lives, believers over the centuries felt constrained either to repress or in some way ignore the black shadow[88]—and with tragic results.

But this bold claim is demonstrably untrue, as we have discovered in the case of Catherine of Siena. No one was more keen than Catherine to affirm that "God is light in whom there is no darkness at all," and yet Catherine (together with other medieval mystics and authors) clearly shows, in both speech and writing, not the least fear or hesitation, but rather an instinctive courage and humility, in openly acknowledging what Jung calls "the dark shadow" and what Catherine calls "the dark of self-knowledge."

---

88. As an aid to the integration of the shadow, the Christ-symbol or Christ-model was of no help, Jung believed, because it excluded completely the dark side of reality: "The Christian image of the self—Christ—lacks the shadow that properly belongs to it" (Jung, *Aion*, 79).

III.
"TO PRAISE, TO BLESS, TO PREACH": CATHERINE'S THREE REMARKABLE FREEDOMS

INTRODUCTION TO PART III
A Motto and Mission

In both word and action, Catherine of Siena made her own the following short text from chapter eight of St. John's Gospel: "You will know the truth, and the truth will set you free" (John 8:32). Catherine, in defense of those men and women whom she found enslaved by their own weakness or by the pernicious lies imposed on them by others, became an outstanding champion of truth. She seized every opportunity she was given to announce to one and all, "The truth will set you free."[1] This insistence on the link between truth and freedom not only marked the Gospel source of Catherine's vision; it also indicated an aspect of her identity as a Dominican. On this subject Yves Congar, the French Dominican theologian, has observed: "A certain mixture of truth and liberty . . . is one of the graces of the Dominican Order."[2] So it was clearly not by accident that, from an early age, Catherine attached herself to an order that had as its primary motto "Veritas" (Truth).[3] All her life, as a free woman dedicated to the Gospel, Catherine lived out her vocation under the sign or rubric of truth.

---

1. See, for example, Letter to Giovanna, Queen of Naples, T 317, *Le Lettere*, vol. 5 (Florence: Giunti, 1940), 49.

2. Yves Congar, "The Order of Preachers in Today's World," *Dominican Ashram* 3, no. 2 (June 1984): 52.

3. The Dominican Mary O'Driscoll, in a work that includes in its title the phrase "Passion for the Truth," remarks: "Catherine's choice of the Dominican Order and, at the same time, her decision not to enter one of its enclosed monasteries are significant. . . . She obviously fell in love with St. Dominic. In her *Dialogue*, she describes him as 'an apostle in the world' who sowed God's word wherever he went, 'dispelling darkness and giving light'" (Mary O'Driscoll, introduction to *Catherine of Siena: Passion for the Truth, Compassion for Humanity*, ed. Mary O'Driscoll [Hyde Park, NY: New City Press, 1993], 8–9. To anyone unfamiliar with the writings of St. Catherine, this work—containing well-chosen, representative passages from the writings of the saint, together with helpful notes and commentary—offers an excellent introduction.

But there was, at that time, another motto associated with the Dominican order: "Laudare, Benedicere, Praedicare"—To Praise, to Bless, to Preach. How this particular motto came to be linked with the Friars Preachers is worth noting. In the early years of the order's existence, an important cleric—a papal legate—at his first encounter with the Friars, was initially shocked by the phenomenon of "this new and unheard-of kind of religious Order."[4] To help himself to come to some definite conclusion about its character—"whether it was from men or from God"—the legate opened a missal "in the name of the Lord" and, on the very first page, he read, "To praise, to bless, to preach." (At that time, this particular phrase formed part of a Preface for the Mass of Our Lady.) The legate, we are told, needed no further sign: "Taking this gladly as an answer from heaven, he was reassured and began to love the Order with all his heart and commended himself to the prayers of the brethren."[5]

The motto "To Praise, to Bless, to Breach," according to the modern Dominican scholar Raimondo Spiazzi, served to indicate the threefold character of the Friars Preachers' vocation: "canonical, priestly, and apostolic."[6] Spiazzi explains why the word "canonical" is apt here. Although the singing of the praises of God ("laudare") is the task of the whole Church, over the centuries different groups of priests and religious have been given this task or have willingly taken it upon themselves as a specific vocation, and many of them have been known as "canons."[7] The second word, "benedicere," refers to the priestly or clerical character of the Dominican order, and in particular to the many

---

4. See Jean de Mailly, "The Life of St. Dominic," in *Early Dominicans: Selected Writings*, ed. Simon Tugwell (New York: Paulist, 1982), 58.

5. De Mailly, *Early Dominicans*, 58.

6. Raimondo Spiazzi, *La Vocazione Domenicana* (Rome: Edizioni San Sisto Vecchio, 1966), 10.

7. Spiazzi, *Vocazione Domenicana*, 20–27.

graces and blessings of Christ that come through the ministry of the sacraments such as Confession and the Eucharist.[8] Finally, "praedicare" refers to the ministry of the Word that has been entrusted in a most particular way to priests belonging to the Order of Preachers.[9]

The interpretation of the Dominican motto given here by Spiazzi is certainly valid. But it is an interpretation that limits the application of the phrase "Laudare, Benedicere, Praedicare" exclusively to the friars in the order, and specifically to those friars ordained to the ministerial priesthood. Might the phrase itself, however, in light of the unique vocation of Catherine of Siena, be given a wider interpretation?

Quite early in the order's life, "Laudare, Benedicere, Praedicare" was referred to in a homily preached by Thomas Agni, the Dominican friar who received Thomas Aquinas into the Order of Preachers. At one point in his homily, Agni offers a sort of working definition of the phrase, explaining it as follows: "*To praise*, that is, in the Divine Office, *to bless* in all one's conversations, and *to preach* among the people and the clergy."[10] Although with this "definition" Agni intends simply to define or describe the life and work of the friars, I propose, in the three chapters that follow, to explore in what sense "Laudare, Benedicere, Praedicare" can be said to also describe the particular Dominican genius and mission of Catherine of Siena.

This mission involved Catherine in a lifelong struggle to liberate people from many different kinds of slavery—from the thrall of evil and oppression, and from lies and fear. But far more

---

8. Spiazzi, *Vocazione Domenicana*, 27–41.
9. Spiazzi, *Vocazione Domenicana*, 41–51.
10. Thomas Agni of Lentini, "A Sermon on St. Dominic," in *Early Dominicans*, 62 (emphasis added).

than the concern—the passion—to free people *from* such things, Catherine's principal focus in both her life and work was directed to what I identified earlier as "freedom *for*." Many times in the *Dialogue*—most notably in *Dialogue* 144—certain sad realities of both sense and spirit are brought into sharp relief, each one of them something from which people need to be liberated: "disordered appetite," "taking pleasure in dishonorable things," "listening judgmentally," "gossiping and being disagreeable," "complaining and judging good deeds as bad and evil ones as good," "insatiable gluttony," and "perverse desire."[11] But, even here, though apparently front and center, freedom *from* is not the exclusive focus.

The faculties of sense and spirit, given their weakened, fallen condition, can indeed draw people down to "the mire and wretchedness."[12] Nevertheless, the life and freedom and energy of the five senses, for example, are clearly to be numbered among God's greatest gifts. Like all our other human faculties, they may require direction and purification. But in Catherine's understanding, they are never to be suppressed out of shame, never to be scorned. Their purpose, as *Dialogue* 144 makes clear, is to offer opportunities for the fullness and greatness of life. Accordingly, the divine Father says to Catherine and, through Catherine, to all believers:

> I gave you eyes to look at the sky and everything else and the beauty of creation through me, and to look at my mysteries. . . . I gave you your ears to listen to my word and to pay heed to your neighbors' needs. I gave you your tongue to proclaim my word,

11. *Dialogue*, no. 144, 300–301.
12. *Dialogue*, no. 144, 300.

to confess your own sins, and to work for the salvation of souls. ... [Your hands] were made to serve your neighbors when you see them sick and to help them with alms in their need. . . . Your feet were given you to serve by carrying your body to places that are holy and useful to you and your neighbors for the glory and praise of my name.[13]

Other statements no less impressive can be found elsewhere in the *Dialogue*. Regarding, for example, the gift to humanity of the created universe, the Father says to Catherine:

I made the heavens and the earth, the sea and the vault of the sky to move above you, the air that you might breathe, fire and water each to temper the other, and the sun so that you would not be left in darkness. All these I made and put in order to serve the needs of humankind. The sky adorned with birds, the earth bringing forth its fruits, the many animals all for the life of humankind, the sea adorned with fish—everything I made with the greatest order and providence.[14]

❀

In the life of Catherine, the first "freedom for" that most immediately impresses us is freedom for the worship of God, the graced capacity to turn to God not out of duty or fear but out of loving reverence and joy. This particular capacity, this breadth and breath of freedom, is something that has been restored to humanity by the "madness" of Christ's Passion and death (Chapter 6, *Laudare*). The second "freedom for" concerns Catherine's relationship with those whom she knew to be among the most wounded and broken in society, and her freedom to move

---

13. *Dialogue*, no. 144, 300.
14. *Dialogue*, no. 140, 288.

among them and bring blessing (Chapter 7, *Benedicere*). The third "freedom for" concerns Catherine's relationship with the social, political, and ecclesiastical world of her time, and the daring nature of the way she felt free, in the cause of justice and right, to address people at all levels of society (Chapter 8, *Praedicare*).

CHAPTER 6
Laudare: Freedom to Praise

1. Catherine at Prayer

"O gentleness of love! How can your bride's heart keep from loving you?"[1] That brief explosion of praise and gratitude occurs in one of Catherine's letters. And there are many similar "explosions" in Catherine's writing, moments when, for the space of a phrase or a sentence or even a whole paragraph, Catherine is so struck by the thought of God's love that she is stunned into prayer.[2] Like almost no other saint I can think of, her thoughts and feelings seem literally to catch fire with sheer wonder. She is, borrowing a phrase from the poet Mary Oliver, "a bride married to amazement."[3] To her friend and spiritual director Raymond of Capua she wrote: "Let our hearts explode wide open, then, as we contemplate a flame and fire of love so great that God has engrafted himself into us and us into himself! O unimaginable love!"[4]

Here what compels Catherine's wonder is the mystery of the Incarnation. But for Catherine, an even greater cause of wonder is the saving event of the Redemption, the mystery of the cross. Once, directly addressing Christ in the *Dialogue*, she exclaims, "O mad lover! It was not enough for you to take on our humanity, you

---

1. Letter to the Superior and Sisters of the Monasteries of Santa Maria delle Vergini and San Giorgio in Perugia, T 217, *Letters*, 2:562.

2. At one point in the *Dialogue* we hear Catherine exclaim: "O immeasurably tender love! Who would not be set afire with such love? What heart could keep from breaking? You, deep well of charity, it seems you are so madly in love with your creatures that you could not live without us!" (*Dialogue*, no. 25, 63).

3. Mary Oliver, "When Death Comes," in *New and Selected Poems* (Boston: Beacon, 1992), 10.

4. Letter to Raymond, T 226, *Letters*, 2:6.

had to die as well!"[5] For Catherine the hope for "our humanity"
is here, a hope realized in the "madness" and magnanimity of
Christ's love: "For he loved us without being loved. Out of love he
created us, and then created us anew to grace in his blood. He gave
his life with such blazing love."[6] On another occasion, meditating
on the mystery of Christ's Passion and death, Catherine finds
herself entering into a form of dialogue with her beloved Savior:

> "Oh my Lord, what a grace it would have been for me if I had
> been some of the stone or soil in which your cross was set, for I
> would have received some of your blood that flowed down from
> the cross!" Gentle First Truth answered: "My dearest daughter,
> you *were* the stone that held me, you and everyone else—I mean
> my love for you—for nothing else could have held me there."[7]

Emboldened by the sheer "madness" of this love, and by the
thought of its saving power, Catherine feels free to sing the praises
of God. For in spite of human weakness, and in spite of the gravity
of sin, somehow the beauty and integrity of created nature—our
soul's "innate liberty"—have been miraculously preserved. Christ
has given us back our freedom. He has released us from our
bondage to sin and death. "You Jesus Christ," Catherine exclaims,
"our reconciler, our refashioner, our redeemer—you, Word and
love, were made our mediator. You turned our great war with God
into a great peace."[8] And again: "You paid the price of your blood

---

5. *Dialogue*, no. 30, 72.

6. Letter to Niccolò Soderini, T 171, *Letters*, 2:26.

7. Letter to Cardinal Orsini, T 223, *Letters*, 2:161–162. To her friend and
disciple Sano di Maco, Catherine writes: "You know that neither nails nor cross
nor rock could have held the God-Man on the cross had not his love for us held him
there" (Letter T 142, *Letters*, 1:76–77).

8. Prayer 1, *Prayers*, 5–6.

when you rescued us from the slavery to sin."[9]

Catherine, when she made this prayer, was absorbed in ecstasy. The date was August 14, 1376, and the place was Avignon. Those friends who were with her at the time described what happened immediately after her prayer was concluded. "She remained as before: silent, motionless, quiet, and absorbed, with her hands spread out and her arms in the form of a cross for an hour or so. Afterwards, holy water was sprinkled on her face and Jesus Christ was invoked over and over. Someone touched her firmly. In a short while the breath began to beat in her and she said several times in a subdued voice, 'Praise to God now and always!' And then, as her breath became stronger, she began to speak more clearly and got up praising and blessing God."[10]

Three years later, on February 15, 1379, Catherine was absorbed in prayer once again. This time she was in Rome, and in a sudden burst of praise she was heard to exclaim, "Your works are wonderful, eternal Trinity!" Later in the prayer, addressing once again the Trinity—and clearly aware that the impulse to praise depends entirely on God, and that, from one perspective, prayer is nothing other than God praying to God,[11]—Catherine exclaims, "Do yourself then offer yourself thanks by giving me the ability to praise you?"[12] Raymond of Capua reports in his *Life* that quite often when Catherine was absorbed in prayer she could be heard praising her divine Lord. He writes: "Catherine was habitually rapt

---

9. Prayer 1, *Prayers*, 7. Catherine speaks elsewhere of the "indescribable love" behind the price paid for our salvation—"love that created us and bought us back not with silver but with blood, and revealed to us our own greatness and our dignity" (Letter to the Defenders of the Commune of Siena, T 123, *Letters*, 2:375).

10. Prayer 1, *Prayers*, 3.

11. Aquinas, commenting on Psalm 39, remarks that since God "the object of our praise" is "greater than all praise," and thus beyond all human strength, "it is fitting to praise God by God" (*unde Deum digne laudare est a Deo*) (*In Psalmos Davidis expositio*, Parma edition, vol. 14, 300).

12. *Orazione XXI, Le Orazioni*, ed. Giuliana Cavallini (Rome: Edizioni Catheriniane, 1978), 246.

out of her bodily senses by the force of her contemplation of the things of God, so that her very body, also, was frequently raised aloft in ecstasy, and there, with the angelic spirits, she joined with the praises of the Lord."[13]

2. Catherine, Mystic of Fire

Rendered speechless on one occasion by the overwhelming intimacy of her contact with God, Catherine, in a letter to Raymond, confesses: "I'm not writing to you about what God has done and is still doing, because there is no language or pen up to the task."[14] But then she adds: "The supreme eternal Word and exalted Godhead gave me such joy that even the parts of my body felt as if they were melting, disintegrating like wax in the fire."[15] These words describe, needless to say, an experience of mystical union at the highest level. But for those still at an earlier stage in the spiritual life, things are different: the fire of divine love is then quite often experienced as a fire of purification. For, as Catherine had come to understand from experience, there is no mysticism without the cross, no intimacy of love without sacrifice.

In the *Dialogue*, the Father declares that those men and women who "run to the table of the most holy cross, in love with

---

13. *Life*, no. 184, 178. Raymond, as friend and spiritual director of Catherine, was a privileged and important witness. But how accurate is the portrait of the saint that he presents in the *Legenda maior*? This question has been raised by a number of modern and contemporary scholars. See, for example, Silvia Nocentini, "The *Legenda maior* of Catherine of Siena," in *A Companion to Catherine of Siena*, eds. Carolyn Muessig, George Ferzoco and Beverly Mayne Kienzle (Boston: Brill, 2012), 343–344. That many things in the *Legenda* fail to measure up to the standards of modern historical research cannot be denied. Raymond was compelled to work within a medieval hagiographical framework. That said, however, for a man of his age, Raymond was remarkable for the effort he made to establish the veracity of the events he records. See Conleth Kearns, "Introduction," in *Life*, xvii.

14. Letter to Raymond, T 226, *Letters*, 2:9.

15. *Letters*, 2:9.

my love," become in time so consumed in the fire of divine charity that they are like burning coals.[16] He says to Catherine that they have become, in effect, "completely set afire in me."[17] And he notes further: "There is no one who can seize them or drag them out of my grace. They have been made one with me and I with them."[18] At this point, it's clear, such men and women experience in depth the serene, unimaginable joy of divine union.

> When they have crossed over and are inebriated with the blood and aflame with the fire of love, they taste in me the eternal Godhead, and I am to them a peaceful sea with which the soul becomes so united that her spirit knows no movement but in me. Though she is mortal she tastes the reward of the immortals, and weighed down still with the body, she receives the lightness of the spirit. Often, therefore, the body is lifted up from the ground because of the perfect union of the soul with me, as if the heavy body had become light.[19]

The impact that an intimate, mystical union can have on the body, as described here, is indeed extraordinary. But far more important for Catherine is the kind of impact it has on the three "powers of the soul" that bear the trace of the Holy Trinity—namely, understanding, memory, and will. These three powers now find themselves utterly and completely free of distraction. "The memory," the Father explains, "finds itself filled with nothing but me. The understanding is lifted up as it gazes into my Truth. The will, which always follows the understanding, loves and unites itself with what the eye of understanding sees."[20]

---

16. *Dialogue*, no. 78, 144–145.
17. *Dialogue*, no. 78, 147.
18. *Dialogue*, no. 78, 147.
19. *Dialogue*, no. 79, 147–148.
20. *Dialogue*, no. 79, 148.

The Father then goes on to describe how, in a truly wondrous manner, the transformed faculties of memory, understanding, and will impact the body. It is one of the most curious and haunting passages in all of Catherine's writing:

> When these powers are gathered and united all together and immersed and set afire in me, the body loses its feeling. For the eye sees without seeing; the ear hears without hearing; the tongue speaks without speaking . . . the hand touches without touching; the feet walk without walking. All the members are bound and busied with the bond and feeling of love.[21]

There are other comparable descriptions in Catherine's writing of high mystical experience, but they are not as numerous as one might expect. Catherine's principal aim in her work is not to speak of the different states of soul that she has attained by God's grace, but rather to point out to others, thirsting for God, the hallowed ordinary way of living faith and love—a plain and illumined Gospel path of prayer.

3. Perseverance in Prayer

The common struggles known to men and women attempting to pray were well-known to Catherine. As a result, Catherine had learned the critical importance of perseverance over the years. In the *Dialogue*, the Father tells her that simple, dogged perseverance in prayer—waiting on God with true self-knowledge and "with a lively faith"—is a most certain way for the soul to attain to "genuine and free love."[22] This message of the Father concerning prayer is a message that we find repeated over and over again by Catherine in her letters:

---

21. *Dialogue*, no. 79, 148.
22. *Dialogue*, no. 65, 122.

You must not break away from holy prayer for any reason except obedience or charity. For often during the time scheduled for prayer the devil comes with all sorts of struggles and annoyances— even more than when you are not at prayer. He does this to make you weary of holy prayer. Often he will say: "This sort of prayer is worthless to you. You should not think about or pay attention to anything except vocal prayer." He makes it seem this way so that you will become weary and confused and abandon the exercise of prayer. But prayer is a weapon with which you can defend yourself against every enemy. If you hold it with love's hand and the arm of free choice, this weapon, with the light of most holy faith, will be your defense.[23]

In a letter to her niece Suora Eugenia, reflecting on the strength and force of those attacks that come during times of prayer, Catherine exhorts the young nun not to be discouraged, but instead, in the face of all the trials and annoyances of the devil, to keep praying: "We shouldn't abandon prayer if we experience many different sorts of struggles in prayer, and spiritual darkness and confusion—when the devil makes it seem that our prayer is not pleasing to God because of all the darkness and confusion. No, we must stand firm, with courage and enduring perseverance."[24]

⚜

Because of the many extraordinary gifts that Catherine possessed throughout her life—gifts of healing, of "reading souls," of fasting to an extreme degree, and of receiving private visions and revelations—we might expect to find in her work a marked emphasis on such extraordinary charismatic phenomena. But, while never dismissing these things out of hand, Catherine insists on and teaches all believers, whatever their state in life, the *ordinary* way of Christian faith and love. Thus, regarding the tendency to focus

---

23. *Dialogue,* no. 65, 122.
24. Letter to Suora Eugenia, T 26, *Letters,* 4:194. See also Letter to Some Novices at Monteoliveto in Perugia, T 203, *Letters,* 4:156.

too much attention on special mystical feelings or experiences in prayer, she writes: "Light seems to be failing us, dazzled as we are by our consolations and the hope we place in revelations—things that do not let us know the truth properly, although we may be acting in good faith."[25]

4. Prayer and the Passion

On Passion Sunday, March 27, 1379, in the presence of a number of her friends and disciples, Catherine fell into an ecstasy. While she was absorbed in prayer, some of the things that came to her lips were faithfully noted down by her friends. As one might expect, this prayer on Passion Sunday is a meditation on the cross. But it has its own unique and distinctive character. According to Suzanne Noffke, "In its theological depth and poetic beauty it far transcends the preoccupation with physical detail that characterizes so much of medieval writing on the subject."[26] The meditation opens with what appears to be an insuperable dilemma. Directly addressing God, Catherine exclaims: "I, mortal lowliness, cannot reach up to your immortal greatness. True, I can experience you through love's energy [through the passion and energy of divine charity], but I cannot see you as you really are."[27] In spite of this acknowledged limitation—the fact of not being able to see God directly in this life—it is for Catherine of enormous import that, already in this life, a true reaching up to God has been made possible because of what she calls "charity's affection." The divine mystery can even now, even here, be seen and known, albeit in a limited form—obscurely, "as in a mirror."

---

25. Letter to Frate Antonio of Nizza, T 328, *Le Lettere*, 5:79.
26. Noffke in *Prayers*, 203.
27. Prayer 19, *Prayers*, 204.

Catherine asks at this point a fundamental question: "When did I become capable of reaching up to your charity's affection?" It's a question that relates to her own faith experience, and it would be natural to expect that, when replying, she would refer back to some intimate spiritual event of grace from the past. But no reference is made by Catherine to any kind of personal contemplative or mystical experience. Instead, she speaks only of the great and saving event of the Incarnation. "When," she asks, "did I become capable of reaching up to your charity's affection? . . . When? When it was time. When the fullness of sacred time had come. . . . When the great doctor came into the world."[28] Catherine then goes on at once to speak of the even greater impact of the event of the cross: "As I see it, it was in this Word's Passion that souls came, by your light, to a perfect knowledge of your charity's affection. For the fire hidden under our ashes began to show itself completely and generously by splitting open his most holy body on the wood of the cross. And it was to draw the soul's affection to higher things, and to bring the mind's eye to gaze into the fire, that your eternal Word wanted to be lifted up high."[29]

Catherine, before the meditation comes to an end, turns her attention to God in a spirit of profound gratitude, and exclaims: "I thank you, I thank you, for you have granted my soul refreshment—in the knowledge you have given me of how I can come to know the exaltedness of your charity even while I am still in my mortal body and in the remedy I see you have ordained to free the world from death."[30]

The message is clear. Instead of relying on mere private, subjective experience, we are asked to focus attention on the reality

---

28. Prayer 19, *Prayers*, 205.
29. *Prayers*, 206.
30. *Prayers*, 215.

of Christ, the incarnate Word, and on the liberating objectivity of Christ's teaching. There are, of course, real contemplative graces, but the bridge that unites us with the Father is not some interior mystical sensation but rather the astonishing sacrificial love of Christ Jesus.

5. Praying the Divine Office

In the period when Catherine was alive the task of praying the Divine Office, though officially a work of the entire Church, was in practice a task reserved almost exclusively to monks, enclosed nuns, and priests. Catherine, being a laywoman and not an enclosed religious, would have had little or no opportunity, therefore, to pray the Divine Office. Instead, she would have been encouraged, together with her companions in the *Mantellate* (most of whom, lacking education, would have been incapable of reading the required Psalms), to recite—over and over again—a number of *Aves* (Hail Marys) and *Paters* (Our Fathers).

But when it came to praising and thanking God, Catherine would not settle for anything but the highest forms of prayer. According to the report of Raymond of Capua, she was determined "to learn to read in order to be able to recite the praises of God and the Hours of the Office."[31] At first, and perhaps not surprisingly, she made little or no progress despite "working hard for several weeks."[32] But Catherine was not prepared to give up on her dream.

So one morning she bowed down before our Lord in prayer and said: "My Lord, if it is your will that I should learn to read, in order

---

31. *Life*, no. 113, 104.
32. *Life*, no. 113, 104.

to be able to sing the Psalms and all your praises in the hours of the Office, please teach me yourself, for of myself I am not able to learn. And if this is not your will, then may your will be done; I will gladly remain illiterate, and will all the more cheerfully devote the time you give me to other kinds of meditation."[33]

Catherine's prayer was not left unheard. To Raymond's astonishment, she was soon able "to read off words with the greatest rapidity,"[34] and "she began to look out for books containing the Divine Office, and would read from them the Psalms, the Hymns, and other parts of the Canonical Hours."[35]

6. Praise of God, Love of Neighbor

"Let's give our neighbors our best efforts, and God our praise."[36] Reading this statement by Catherine, one might presume she was referring to two separate things: our duty on the one hand to care for our neighbors in need, and our duty on the other to give due honor and praise to God. But are these two distinct dimensions of life really separate in Catherine's understanding? Are they not decisively linked? However we decide to answer this question, there is one thing that cannot be ignored, and that is the great and simple truth announced over and over again in her letters: "We owe God glory and praise, in love, for his name."[37]

God has given us love and God has given us honor. For he loved us before we even existed. And in his Son's blood, in which we have received the fruit of grace, he has honored us by taking away

---

33. *Life*, no. 113, 104–105.
34. *Life*, no. 113, 105.
35. *Life*, no. 113, 105.
36. Letter to Nicola da Osimo, T 181, *Letters*, 1:256.
37. Letter to the Defenders of the People and City of Siena, T 311, *Letters*, 4:307.

the disgrace into which we had fallen because of Adam's sin. This was the greatest benefit we could possibly receive, since it freed us from death and gave us life. So we owe God honor and love.[38]

God's name, we know, is honored in a wonderful way in the Divine Liturgy. But is it possible that some further way of honoring and loving God is being asked of us? Given the spontaneity and freedom with which God first loved us, is it possible, according to Catherine's way of thinking, that we are now being asked to love in that same extraordinary way? At first glance, it would seem to be out of the question, since God as God has absolutely no need of our human love. Yet in the *Dialogue*, the Father says to Catherine: "I ask you to love me with the same love with which I love you. But for me you cannot do this, for I have loved you without being loved."[39] This thought is then developed a further step: "Whatever love you have for me you owe me, so you love me not gratuitously but out of duty, while I love you not out of duty but gratuitously. So you cannot give me the kind of love I ask of you."[40]

What, then, is the solution? Is there a way in which infinite love can be answered by mere finite human love? The reply Catherine hears at this point in the *Dialogue* is startling and yet familiar. It contains both the surprise and the authority of the Gospel: "This is why I have put you among your neighbors: so that you can do for them what you cannot do for me—that is, love them without any concern for thanks and without looking for any profit for yourself. And whatever you do for them I will consider done for me."[41] This message is one we find repeated many times

---

38. Letter to the Defenders of the People and City of Siena, T 311, *Letters*, 4:307–308.
39. *Dialogue*, no. 64, 121.
40. *Dialogue*, no. 64, 121.
41. *Dialogue*, no. 64, 121.

in Catherine's letters.[42] By showing kindness to our neighbors, by offering (for example) "material help with a great and generous heart," we not only love God but "give God the blossoms of glory and praise."[43]

7. Freedom from False Forms of Religion

Devoted service to people in need should, one imagines, be central to the lives of those men and women who have taken vows of religion. But, sad to say, according to the *Dialogue*, the reality is that in religious life there are individuals who use the basic practices of religion, such as attendance at the Divine Office, to give themselves an excuse for not attending to the needs of those around them. In the words of God the Father:

> These people find all their pleasure in seeking their own spiritual consolation—so much so that often they see their neighbors in spiritual or temporal need and refuse to help them. Under pretense of virtue they say, "It would make me lose my spiritual peace and quiet, and I would not be able to say my Hours [of the Divine Office] at the proper time." Then if they do not enjoy consolation they think they have offended me. But they are deceived by their own spiritual pleasure, and they offend me more by not coming to the help of their neighbors' need than if they had abandoned all their consolations. . . . For in charity for their neighbors they find me, but in their own pleasure, where they are seeking me, they will be deprived of me.[44]

---

42. In one letter to a group of women disciples in Siena, for example, Catherine writes: "You will see that there is no service you can do for God, and so you will extend your love to your neighbors, doing for them the service you cannot do for God. You will visit the sick, help the poor, and console those who are troubled" (Letter to Certain of her Daughters in Siena, T 40, *Letters*, 2:409).

43. Letter to Countess Bandeçça Salimbeni, T 113, *Letters*, 2:680.

44. *Dialogue*, no. 69, 130–131.

These individuals appear to be at one with "the color" of the particular order to which they belong, but in fact they are held fast by the chain of "old customs."[45] Outside they look authentic, but inside they become cold-hearted and judgmental. They are "more concerned about observing the ceremonies of the rule than the rule itself. And often for want of light they are quick to fall into judging those who observe the rule more perfectly than they do, though they may be less perfect in all the ceremonies of which their judges are so observant."[46] In this context, the advice Catherine gives to one of her fellow *Mantellate*, Daniella of Orvieto, is significant. Daniella had written to say that she was feeling called by God to respond to people in need of help. But if she did this, she would no longer be able to fulfill a spiritual promise that she had made sometime earlier. What should she do? Catherine's reply to Daniella merits—for a number of reasons—to be cited at length. It reveals not only a clear Gospel spirit and great practical wisdom but also a notable kindness and tenderness of heart.

> I gather from your letter that you are apparently upset—not just a little but perhaps more than ever before. On the one hand you feel God is spiritually calling you in new ways, and yet God's servants take the opposite position, saying it's not good. I have plenty of compassion for you, for I know of no greater distress than this. . . . You can't resist God, but you would like to do as God's servants say, trusting in their light and knowledge more than in your own—and yet you seem unable to do so. Now I am answering you simply, according to my own limited and lowly view, and not imposing anything at all on you in any definitive way. I say only, respond to whatever you feel called to that doesn't

---

45. *Dialogue*, no. 162, 351.
46. *Dialogue*, no. 162, 351. See also T 316, *Letters*, 3:330.

come from yourself. So, if you see souls in danger and you can help them, don't close your eyes but with thorough concern try to help them, even to the point of death. And don't worry about your resolutions, whether about silence or anything else, so that it won't be said to you later, "Cursed be you who kept silent!" Our entire principle and foundation is laid only in charity for God and for our neighbors; all other practices are instruments. . . . Never let love for the instrument or the building make you abandon the principal foundation, God's honor and love for your neighbors.[47]

Statements such as these, and other quotes above from the *Dialogue,* are not intended in any way to minimize the importance of the ordinary forms of ascetic and religious practice—the maintenance of a spirit of recollection, for example, or for those committed to religious life, regular attendance at monastic choir. Catherine, writing to a young Dominican friar whom she had helped convert to a good life, points out that if he wants to direct his life to God and "do everything for the glory and praise of God's name," it won't be possible unless he willingly submits to the common discipline of religious life. "You won't be able to do any of this," she declares, "if you go gadding about in all sorts of socializing, staying away from your cell and absenting yourself from choir."[48]

Should the issue, however, concern those people who are spending themselves for the Church and giving their best for God's people, far from criticizing them, Catherine shows she is

47. Letter to Daniella of Orvieto, T 316, *Letters*, 3:330. It's clear from this passage that Catherine possessed to an impressive degree the gift of wise discernment or what she calls "discrezione." This gift of discernment, based on self-knowledge, allows the individual to maintain a proper balance in the search for perfection, protecting him or her from pursuing extremes of any kind. For the most helpful, most complete study of this aspect of Catherine's teaching, see Ragazzi, *Obeying the Truth.*
48. Letter to Frate Matteo di Francesco Tolomei, T 94, *Letters*, 2:673.

willing to support and defend them in every possible way. Because of the busy lives they lead, these individuals can sometimes feel bereft of ordinary spiritual consolation. Unable to keep to fixed or regular hours, they often find they are no longer able to enjoy a calm and peaceful spirit at the time of prayer. And that, of course, can be discouraging. But not for a moment should they lose heart, Catherine declares:

> Although we may be deprived of the consolation of reciting the office and all the psalms, or of saying them at the proper time and place with the calm mind we would like to have, this does not mean our time is wasted. This is, in fact, also working for God. So you shouldn't worry about it, especially when you are working and wearing yourself out in the service of Christ's bride.[49]

Here, as so often in her reflections on life and liturgy, Catherine strikes the note of freedom: freedom, first of all, to praise and worship God in the Divine Office, but freedom also to honor God by devoting wholehearted attention to our neighbors in need, giving them the best of our efforts.

---

49. Letter to Nicola da Osimo, T 282, *Letters*, 2:683.

CHAPTER 7
Benedicere: Freedom to Bless

1. Meeting Catherine

There is perhaps no better starting point for a reflection on "Benedicere," as it relates to Catherine of Siena, than Thomas Agni's brief prescription: "To bless in all one's conversations." That being the case, one question must be asked: What was it like, in practice, to hold a conversation with Catherine of Siena? Of all the different ways one might choose to approach this question, the best by far, I would suggest, is to take up and read Catherine's letters. For it is in her letters that the distinctive cadence of her voice and the unique character of her message are most in evidence: "I, Catherine, servant and slave of God's servants, am writing to *encourage* you . . ."[1]

To all the different friends and associates who surrounded her during her short life, Catherine was able to communicate with manifest ease a vital sense of their own human dignity and worth. This was due, in part, to the profundity of her message—the wisdom and grace of the Gospel itself—but it was also related to the fine instinct she possessed for delivering a straightforward, illuminating word of encouragement just when it was needed. Like very few other authors of the Middle Ages, Catherine of Siena comes across in almost everything she says or writes with an almost startling vividness. Reading her work today we cannot help but wonder what it must have been like to meet her in person.

Raymond of Capua, her great friend and the man who knew her perhaps better than anyone else, tells us that even though

---

1. Letter to Frate Bartolomeo Dominici, T 200, *Letters*, 1:21 (emphasis added).

Catherine's writings are clearly impressive, they must take "second place" to what he calls "her living words as they came from her lips during her lifetime."[2] He writes: "For the Lord had endowed her with a most ready tongue, a charisma of utterance adapted to every circumstance, so that her words burnt like a torch and none who ever heard her could escape being touched."[3] And there was something else about Catherine that Raymond admits can hardly be put into words. He writes:

> My heart overflows as I recall it and compels me to record here this mysterious attraction which was part of her. It made itself felt, not only by her spoken word, but by the very fact of one being present where she was. By it she drew the souls of men to the things of God and made them take delight in God himself. She drove out despondency from the hearts of any who shared her company, and banished dejection of spirit and all feelings of depression, bringing in instead a peace of soul so deep and so unwonted that those who experienced it did not know themselves.[4]

"What a fascination she exercised!"[5] Raymond exclaims in the same passage, recalling the impact Catherine made on so many people during her life. No small part of that "fascination" has survived in the letters, and particularly in those letters in which Catherine's gift for encouraging the weak and the despondent is most in evidence. In this regard, some of the things she wrote to her friend, the poet Neri dei Pagliaresi, are especially worthy of note. When Catherine died, Neri was inconsolable. In his grief, he composed a poem that, in one short stanza, affords us a vivid, intimate portrait of his much-missed friend. The stanza contains

---

2. *Life*, no. 9, 8.
3. *Life*, no. 9, 8.
4. *Life*, no. 27, 28.
5. *Life*, no. 27, 28.

a list of some of the ways in which Catherine had sought to bring to her poet-friend the blessing of much-needed encouragement over the years.

> Tell me, who will save me now from an evil end?
> Who will preserve me from delusions?
> Who will guide me when I try to climb?
> Who will console me now in my distress?
> Who will ask me now: "Are you not well?"
> Who will persuade me that I shall not be damned?[6]

Numbered among Catherine's disciples was another young man much given to melancholy and self-doubt, a Dominican friar named Simone da Cortona. Oppressed by temptation and weakness, Simone had begun to fear that God had somehow turned against him: "For a long time already I've found myself canceled, erased, deleted from the book in which I used to feel so sweetly nourished."[7] Catherine, hearing of his distress, writes to the young Dominican, pointing out that it is the devil who has put "these illusory thoughts and suggestions into our heart" so that "we think we have been rejected by God."[8] "This leads to discouragement," she explains, "which in turn makes us give up the practice of prayer because we imagine God does not find us acceptable—and we have become so despondent we can't stand ourselves."[9]

---

6. Stanza from a poem by Neri dei Pagliaresi, cited in Arrigo Levasti, *My Servant Catherine,* trans. D.M. White (London: Blackfriars, 1954), 110.

7. Frate Simone da Cortona, Letter VIII, *Lettere dei Discepoli di Santa Caterina,* appended to *Le Lettere,* vol. 6 (Florence: Giunti, 1940), 61. Although in *Le Lettere dei Discepoli* the letter is attributed to an "Anonimo," Noffke for good reason believes that the author is Frate Simone. The letter itself is addressed to Neri dei Pagliaresi.

8. Letter to Frate Simone da Cortona, T 56, *Letters,* 2:574.

9. *Letters,* 2:574.

The solution, Catherine urges (revealing once again the *objectivity* of her vision and spirituality), is for the young man to recall to mind the fact that "the Son gave his life for us to restore us to grace; he made his blood a bath for us to wash away the leprosy of our wickedness."[10] If we should ignore or forget that saving memory, Catherine notes, we'll begin to lose hope and become "so cowardly that we'll be afraid of our own shadow!"[11] What is it, Catherine asks, that we need, then? Her answer: "We need Christ's blood!"[12] What she means by this bold declaration is that we need knowledge—living knowledge—of God's unconditional love for us: "In that blood we will discover a firm confidence that will free us of all slavish fear."[13]

Frate Simone, in the throes of depression, had written earlier: "I am not signing my name, because I don't know that I have a name."[14] Catherine, at the close of her letter to Simone, writes: "I long to see you bathed, drowned in the blood of Christ crucified. And I am telling you that then you will have a name, and I will have found my son again! So bathe, drown yourself, in the blood, without discouragement, without despondency!"[15]

2. Vision of God, Vision of Neighbor

Not only was Catherine able to offer hope to those among her contemporaries who had begun to lose their own, she had a striking ability, at the same time, to alert the most wounded and unhappy of people to a depth within them—a depth they had

---

10. Letter to Frate Simone da Cortona, T 56, *Letters*, 2:574.
11. *Letters*, 2:574.
12. *Letters*, 2:574.
13. *Letters*, 2:574.
14. Frate Simone da Cortona, Letter to Neri dei Pagliaresi, *Lettere dei Discepoli*, VIII, 62.
15. Letter to Frate Simone da Cortona, T 56, *Letters*, 2:575.

never suspected—of real or potential integrity and beauty. This gift, this bright perception, had its origin in something more than Catherine's natural kindness, as is made clear in the *Dialogue* and elsewhere. In the *Dialogue*, the Father says to her: "Open your mind's eye and look within me, and you will see the dignity and beauty of my reasoning creature."[16] These are words of radiant promise. Catherine, by simply lifting up her mind and heart to the Father, contemplating in faith the marvel of his "fiery and consuming love," discovers not only a vision of God and a vision of herself in God, but also a new and compassionate vision and understanding of her neighbor: "The love the soul sees that God has for her, she in turn extends to all other creatures. And what is more, she immediately feels compelled to love her neighbor as herself, for she sees how supremely she herself is loved by God, beholding herself in the wellspring of the sea of the divine essence."[17]

What is immediately clear from these lines is that the source of Catherine's vision of the neighbor, and the cause of her deep respect for the individual person, is at its core a contemplative experience. What she receives when in prayer and contemplation is not simply the command from God to love her neighbor as she had been loved, but an unforgettable insight beyond or beneath the symptoms of human distress, a glimpse into the hidden grace and dignity of each individual person. So deeply affected was Catherine by this vision of the neighbor that she remarked once

---

16. *Dialogue*, no. 1, 26.

17. Letter to Raymond, T 226, *Le Lettere*, 3:297. Elsewhere, on the same theme, Catherine writes: "God loves people above all else, and that is why God's servants love other people so much—because they see that the Creator loves them above all else. I love what the person I love loves. That is the nature of love" (T 16, *Letters*, 2:116). In a letter to a woman named Monna Agnesa Catherine speaks of "the wise person" who, having come to know the amazing love that God has for us, "falls in love with God and with what God loves most, human beings" (T 340, *Letters*, 3:306).

to Raymond of Capua that if he could only see this beauty—the inner, hidden beauty—of the individual person as she saw it, he would be willing to suffer and die for it. "Oh Father . . . if you were to see the beauty of the human soul, I am convinced that you would willingly suffer death a hundred times, were it possible, in order to bring a single soul to salvation. Nothing in this world of sense around us can possibly compare in loveliness with a human soul."[18]

3. Identification with Sinners

St. Catherine's deeply passionate concern for the salvation of others was so radical at times that it had the effect of making her spend a considerable amount of time with disgraced sinners, down-and-outs, and criminals. Raymond criticized her on occasion for the kind of company she was keeping. Catherine, by way of response, felt it necessary to explain to Raymond what she called her "secret." She told him how once, lifted up like St. Paul in ecstasy, "I saw the secret things of God, things which it is not given to any pilgrim here below to utter."[19] She thought, in fact, she was in heaven already and that she could remain there in bliss forever. But her "Eternal Spouse" said to her: "You must go back; the salvation of many souls demands it. It demands, too, a radical change in the way of life that has been yours up to this. Your cell [a room in Catherine's house] will no longer be your dwelling-place. . . . You will even have to leave your own city. But I will be with you always."[20] From this point on, Catherine's only consolation in life was in seeking out the lost. "Father, now that I have let you into my secret," she remarked to Blessed Raymond, "I know it will

---

18. *Life*, no. 151, 146.
19. *Life*, no. 213, 202.
20. *Life*, no. 216, 204–205.

keep you from ever taking part with those who denounce me for that openness of spirit with which I freely welcome all the souls who come my way."[21]

Not all religious people, it has to be said, are noted for such openness of spirit, such imaginative kindness. Thomas Merton, taking his cue from a novel by Fyodor Dostoevsky, paints a picture of two very different types of people in religious life. He speaks of an "eternal conflict in monasticism—and doubtless in Christianity itself"; a conflict, that is, "between the rigid, authoritarian, self-righteous, ascetic Therapont, who delivers himself from the world by sheer effort, and then feels qualified to call down curses upon it; and the Staretz Zossima, the kind, compassionate man of prayer who identifies himself with the sinful and suffering world in order to call down God's blessing upon it."[22]

Clearly Catherine belongs to the Zossima camp. Like the wise and humble Staretz, her whole concern is to call down a blessing and not a curse on humanity. Accordingly, with words of naked appeal, she cries out to God: "O high eternal Trinity! . . . Turn the eye of your mercy on your creatures. I know that mercy is your hallmark, and no matter where I turn I find nothing but your mercy. That is why I run crying to your mercy to have mercy on the world."[23] At one point in the *Dialogue*, with an even greater sense of urgency, she exclaims: "O depth of love! What heart could keep from breaking at the sight of your greatness descending to the lowliness of our humanity? . . . In the name of this unspeakable

---

21. *Life*, no. 216, 205. With regard to the voices of opposition within Siena, Catherine writes: "I'm sorry about the energy and effort my fellow citizens are spending in worrying and wagging their tongues over me. It seems they have nothing else to do but speak ill of me and the company that is with me" (T 123, *Letters*, 2:377).

22. Thomas Merton, *Contemplative Prayer* (New York: Herder, 1969), 30–31.

23. Prayer 9, *Prayers*, 72.

love, then, I beg you—I would force you even—to have mercy on your creatures."[24]

Certain aspects of Catherine's relationship with William Flete, an ascetic Englishman who lived as a hermit in the forest of Lecceto, are reminiscent of the conflict between the two Russian monks, Zossima and Therapont. Although famous for his austerities and the holiness of his life, William was also, it would appear, "a very impatient and somewhat intolerant person, given to carping criticism."[25] In one of the letters Catherine wrote to William, she upbraids him for what she calls his tendency towards "gossip" and "rash judgment."[26] She writes: "My heart and my soul grieve to see you wrong the perfection to which God has called you, under the pretense of love and virtue."[27]

Catherine points out to William that mortifying the body is not "the chief aim." What, then, is the aim? It is, she says, to serve God and neighbor "from pure love."[28] Those who divest themselves of the old man, and array themselves in the new man, Christ Jesus, following him manfully, "rejoice in everything."[29]

> They do not make themselves judges of the servants of God, or of any other rational creature, but rejoice in every situation, and in every form of living that they see, saying, "Thanks to you, Eternal Father, that you have so many mansions in your house!" And they are happier with the different forms of living than if they were to

---

24. *Dialogue*, no. 13, 50.

25. Comment by Vida D. Scudder in *Saint Catherine of Siena as Seen in Her Letters*, 57.

26. Letter to William Fleet, T 64, *Le Lettere*, 1:243.

27. *Le Lettere*, 1:243. To another hermit, a friend of William's and one of her own disciples, Catherine writes: "I feel an intolerable anguish of heart when I see God being offended so openly under color of virtue, in spite of the fact that we can never and must never judge any creature's intention; even if we know of a fault or actually witness it, we must not judge the intention, but bear it with great compassion before God; to do the opposite is to be deceived by our own opinions" (G 130, *I, Catherine*, 229).

28. G 130, *I, Catherine*, 241.

29. G 130, *I, Catherine*, 241.

see everyone walking the same way, for thus they see the greatness of God's goodness more manifest. They find joy in everything, taking from everything the fragrance of the rose. And, even as to a thing which they may expressly see to be a sin, they do not pass judgment, but regard it rather with holy true compassion, saying, "Today it's your turn, and tomorrow mine, unless it be for divine grace which preserves me.[30]

Addressing the same theme in a letter sent to Caterina di Ghetto, one of the *Mantellate* at Siena, Catherine writes: "See that you don't act like those stupid and senseless people who want to appoint themselves as both investigators and judges of what God's servants do and how they live. . . . Realize that wanting to make God's servants walk the same way we do is nothing less than an attempt to regulate and legislate for the Holy Spirit."[31]

Another individual with whom Catherine corresponded on this question was her friend Daniella from Orvieto. In some ways, Daniella was the feminine equivalent of Brother William, especially in her attitude to the perceived weaknesses of others. Catherine complains to Daniella about this "presumption."[32] In the same letter, however, Catherine confesses that, in the past, she too was guilty of judging others harshly. "Wretch that I am . . . I've so often fallen into . . . passing judgment on my neighbors."[33] Such clear identification with the weakness of the person to whom she is writing reveals in Catherine a noteworthy humility, but also a fine sense of tact, an instinct for disarming any potential distress or anger that might be caused by her words. Catherine loved the truth with a passion, and she loved proclaiming it, but she also knew how dangerous and hurtful truth can be if not accompanied

---

30. G 130, *I, Catherine*, 242.
31. Letter to Caterina di Ghetto, T 50, *Letters*, 2:595.
32. Letter to Daniella of Orvieto, T 65, *Letters*, 3:238.
33. *Letters*, 3:240.

by basic kindness and by what she calls "congeniality." To her hermit friend Frate Felice da Massa, she wrote: "Let the truth be your delight; let it always be in your mouth and proclaim it when it is needed. Proclaim it lovingly and to everyone, especially to those you love with a special love—but with a certain congeniality [*con una piacevolezza*], putting the shortcomings of the other person on your own shoulders. If in the past you haven't done it as sensitively as you should, let's do better in the future."[34]

4. Catherine's "heresy"

Although Catherine found time during her life for encounters with religious-minded people such as William Flete, Daniella of Orvieto, and Frate Felice, she also made time to meet and talk with lepers, prisoners, public sinners, and prostitutes—people regarded by most of society as outcasts. Owing to this "scandalous" behavior, complaints were constantly being made against Catherine. She had multiple detractors. There was, however, one man among her contemporaries who spoke out powerfully in her defense. His name was Don Giovanni dalle Celle. In answer to an accusation that he had been guilty of attacking the young mystic, Giovanni wrote: "Not only do I not want to do such a thing, but I am prepared to die for her honor."[35] Then, referring to Catherine's very open, very public identification with sinners—Catherine's "heresy," he called it—Giovanni declared: "I would consider it a glory to be called a heretic with her."[36]

O sweetest heresy of the heavenly Catherine! You turn sinners into just people. Friend of publicans and sinners, you make the

---

34. Letter to Frate Felice da Massa, T 51, *Letters*, 2:638.
35. Giovanni delle Celle, cited by Noffke in *Letters*, 2:532.
36. *Letters*, 2:532.

angels laugh and heaven rejoice. You honor God; you enlighten the Church of Christ; you raise the dead to spiritual life. . . . You have the words of eternal life, and we have believed and known that you are anointed by the Holy Spirit and are the daughter of the living God![37]

The driving force behind Catherine's great magnanimity was, as noted earlier, her contemplative courage, her willingness to raise what she calls the eye of her understanding above herself "to meet the look of ineffable divine charity with which God gazed [on her]."[38] "Love," she wrote to a Dominican friar, "is the explanation of all this." Just as the desire of Christ—the "eye" of Christ—was "fixed entirely on his Father's honor," she wants the Dominican to be likewise conformed: "For then you will become one with him and have a share in his great-heartedness and not be narrow and constricted. I tell you again that unless a soul raises itself up and opens its eye to focus it on the boundless goodness and love God has shown for his creature, it can never attain to this greatness of soul but will remain instead so narrow and constricted it will have no room either for self or neighbor."[39]

One example of Catherine's own greatness of spirit concerns a man she came to know in Siena, a young, headstrong aristocrat called Francesco Malavolti. Before they met, Francesco—by his own honest admission—had been "living lasciviously and unrestrainedly in the wretched delights of the world and the flesh," behaving, he says, "as though I were never to die, recklessly pursuing my inordinate lusts with all my power."[40] But after his first encounter with Catherine, he went "from being a bestial man

37. Giovanni delle Celle, cited by Noffke in *Letters,* 2:532.
38. Letter to Frate Bartolomeo Dominici, T 204, *Le Lettere,* 3:197.
39. *Le Lettere,* 3:198–199.
40. Francesco Malavolti, "Il Processo Castellano," in *Fontes Vitae S. Catharinae Senensis Historici,* vol. 9, ed. M.H. Laurent (Milan: Fratelli Bocca, 1942), 377.

and well-nigh demoniacal"—again his own words—to attaining, we are told, to "true knowledge and life according to the Spirit."[41]

His conversion, however, was by no means easy or automatic. And, much to the embarrassment of some of Catherine's followers, Francesco, closely identified at this stage with the pious group, fell back into his old ways. On one particular occasion, this occurred during one of Catherine's absences from Siena. When Catherine returned, Francesco, because of the shame and disgrace he was feeling, refused to meet face to face with his friend. But she, wounded to the heart by Francesco's unhappy isolation and sense of failure, wrote to him as follows:

> Dearest and more than dearest son in Christ gentle Jesus . . . it seems to me that the devil has you so stolen away that, once again, he will not let you be found. I, your wretched mother, go around searching for you and sending for you, because I would like to place you up on the shoulders of my sorrow and compassion. . . . So, open the eye of your mind, dearest son, look up from the darkness. Acknowledge your guilt, not with confusion of mind but with self-knowledge and hope in God's goodness. . . . Don't let the devil deceive you by either fear or shame. . . . Come, come, dearest son! Well may I call you dear, for you have cost me so much in tears, sweat, and bitter care.[42]

Who could resist such an appeal? Francesco went immediately to meet Catherine, though not, he tells us, without great fear and shame.

> But she, like the kindest and sweetest mother, received me with a joyful countenance, giving the greatest comfort to my weakness.

---

41. Malavolti, *Fontes Vitae S. Catharinae Senensis Historici*, 384.
42. Letter to Francesco Malavolti, T 45, *Le Lettere*, 1:178–180.

And a few days afterwards, when I went to her again, and one of the virgin's woman companions said to her, in a rather querulous manner, that I had little stability, she said with a smile: "Never mind, my sisters. . . . I shall put such a yoke [the marriage symbol] upon his neck that he will never be able to slip out of it." Since, at this time, I had both wife and children, the sisters, and I with them, laughed at these words, and we made merry, nor did any of us then think any more about them.[43]

Over the years, a considerable number of commentators have tried to present Catherine as a great lover of nature and even as a poet of nature like St. Francis of Assisi.[44] But, frankly, I am not convinced. What holds Catherine's attention is not so much natural creation, but people, human beings—or as she would say herself, "the beauty of the rational creature." Catherine is the saint not of nature, but of human nature. She is the saint of our humanity.

---

43. Malavolti, "Il Processo Castellano," 379–380.
44. See Drane, *History of St. Catherine,* 162–163.

CHAPTER 8
Praedicare: Freedom to Preach

1. An Unexpected Vocation

How was it that a young laywoman with almost no education found herself at the very heart of the society of her day, speaking with a force and authority considered by most to belong only to ordained preachers and only to men? Here, the first thing to note is that the call to this way of life came to Catherine herself as an enormous surprise. For a number of years, she had been contentedly pursuing a hidden, contemplative life in her parents' house with no expectation whatever of any kind of external preaching apostolate. But then, one day, according to the report of Blessed Raymond, Christ appeared to her in a vision, declaring that she must change her life completely: "You must now begin to bear fruit not only in yourself but in other souls as well."[1]

At first, Catherine was utterly bewildered by this visitation, fearing that it might mark the end of her contemplative intimacy with God. But Christ said:

> I have no intention whatever of parting you from myself, but rather of making sure to bind you to me all the closer. . . . Remember that I have laid down two commandments of love: love of me and love of your neighbor. . . . On two feet you must walk my way; on two wings you must fly to heaven.[2]

---

1. *Life*, no. 121, 116.
2. *Life*, no. 121, 116.

At this point in the conversation, Christ reveals a detail about an early desire of Catherine that is astonishing. Apparently, so great was Catherine's desire to be a preacher that she was prepared, if necessary, to disguise herself as a man!

> Remember how you used to plan to put on man's attire and enter the Order of Preachers in foreign parts to labor for the good of souls. Remember how, from that time forward, you burned with eagerness to put on the habit which you now wear, so as to satisfy your loving devotion to my faithful servant Dominic, who founded his Order above all to labor zealously for souls. Why then are you surprised, why are you sad, because I am now drawing you to the work which you have longed for since your infancy?[3]

Although Catherine was "somewhat heartened" by this reply, she went on to say at once:

> But may I ask you, Lord, if it not be presumptuous, how can what you say be done? How can one like me, feeble and of no account, do any good for souls? My very sex, as I need not tell you, puts many obstacles in the way. The world has no use for women in such work as that, and propriety forbids that a woman mix so freely in the company of men.[4]

Before proceeding further with Catherine's reported dialogue, it is worth asking if the statements about womanish frailty, attributed here to Catherine—statements clearly shocking to the modern ear—represent Catherine's own thinking on the topic, or if her words perhaps were filtered through the lens of an inherited misogyny in Raymond of Capua's thinking. Well, the answer,

---

3. *Life*, no. 121, 116.
4. *Life*, no. 121, 116.

unfortunately, is that Catherine, as a woman of her age, absorbed the common view of that time—a view that nowadays would certainly be regarded as sexist. Writing, for example, to Giovanna, Queen of Naples, and exhorting her to change her way of thinking about Pope Urban VI, Catherine declares that if she would only do the right thing, and learn to be strong and unwavering, she would lose "the condition of being a woman" and would become instead "a virile man."[5] In similar vein, writing in a letter to three widows living at Naples, Catherine declares: "Be steady and firm. Don't follow the womanish nature that flaps about like a leaf in the wind but be manly and constant in proclaiming that Pope Urban VI truly is the pope, Christ's vicar on earth."[6]

Although, on the evidence of these statements, Catherine was by no means free of the widespread and unhappy misogynism of her time,[7] she was able nevertheless to transcend the restricted roles usually assigned to women, whether they were religious or lay—a fact that Raymond was happy to record over and over again in his *Life*. But initially, the role she was being asked by Christ to undertake—a dramatic, public apostolate—must have seemed impossible. She was a woman, a young woman, and so perceived generally at that time as "feeble and of no account."[8] How could

---

5. Letter to Giovanna, Queen of Naples, T 312, *Le Lettere* 5:13.

6. Letter to Three Widows of Naples, T 356, *Letters*, 4:292. On another occasion, Catherine, exasperated with Raymond because of his refusal to risk martyrdom, exclaimed: "You were a man when you assured me of your willingness to suffer for God's honor; now, when it comes to setting the nail, don't show me that you're a woman!" (T 344, *Letters*, 4:234).

7. On a totally different topic, that of the Crusades, Catherine reveals herself to be once again very much a woman of her age. Kenelm Foster remarks: "As a woman of her time she thought it the plain duty of a Christian knight to be ready to draw his sword for the recovery of the holy places—which, by right, she said, 'belong to us.' Nevertheless, she could say of the Muslims, 'they are our brothers, redeemed by the blood of Christ just as we are'—a remarkable statement for that time." See Foster, introduction to *I, Catherine*, 25.

8. *Life*, no. 121, p.116.

she even consider, therefore, undertaking such a task? When Catherine had finished voicing her alarm, Christ immediately responded, offering the following calm and serene answer to all her doubts and queries:

> Was it not I who created the human race? Male and female I created them. Does it not depend on my own will where I shall pour out my grace? With me there is no longer male and female, nor lower class and upper class; for all stand equal in my sight, and all things are equally in my power to do. . . . Why then do you hesitate about the *how*? Do you think that I lack the knowledge or the power to choose the manner in which what I have decreed and planned is to be carried out? However, I know it is humility that makes you speak like this, and not lack of faith, so I will explain. At the present day human pride has passed beyond all bounds, especially the pride of those who regard themselves as wise and learned men. My justice can no longer refrain from putting them back in their place by a just judgment.[9]

The kind of opposition that St. Catherine had to confront in the fourteenth century, St. Teresa of Avila also had to endure two centuries later. In *The Book of Her Life*, Teresa complains that when someone like herself was moved by a "loving impulse" to speak out on an important issue, at once "a thousand persecutions" would rain down on her head.[10] She would be accused, once it was known that she was "a woman," of "lacking in humility" and of having the audacity "to teach the one from whom she should

---

9. *Life*, no. 122, 116–117.
10. St Teresa of Avila, *The Book of Her Life*, ch. 20, no. 24, in *The Collected Works of St. Teresa of Avila*, vol. 1, *The Book of Her Life, Spiritual Testimonies and the Soliloquies*, trans. Kieran Kavanaugh and Otilio Rodriquez (Washington, DC: ICS, 1976), 183.

be learning."[11] Greatly troubled by this situation, Teresa began to wonder if perhaps what the men were telling her was correct, and that it would be wise, therefore, to follow "what St. Paul said about the enclosure of women" and never to go out at all, but instead "be always occupied in prayer."[12] This proposal may sound to some ears wise and traditional. But the Lord, not willing to entertain for a moment the decidedly strict, limiting advice Teresa had received from the men, declared: "Tell them they shouldn't follow just one part of Scripture but that they should look at other parts, and ask them if they can by chance tie my hands."[13]

One brief but illuminating part of Scripture that those opposed to the active apostolates of both Teresa and Catherine might well have consulted for their benefit are those texts in the New Testament that speak of a woman—Mary Magdalene—as the first witness to the Resurrection. Later Christian tradition would not hesitate to speak of Magdalene as "the Apostle to the Apostles." And Catherine herself, in a passing reference in one of her earliest letters, happily makes reference to "that loving apostle, Magdalene."[14] Inspired presumably by an early legend concerning the saint, Catherine speaks of Mary Magdalene as a woman so "drunk with love for her Master" that "after his holy resurrection she preached in the city of Marseilles."[15] It was, without question, that same "drunkenness" that led the young Catherine to dare

---

11. St. Teresa of Avila, *The Book of Her Life*, ch. 20, no. 24, 183.

12. St. Teresa of Avila, "Spiritual Testimonies," no. 15, in *Collected Works*, vol. 1, 393.

13. St. Teresa of Avila, *Collected Works*, vol. 1, 393.

14. Letter to Monna Agnese Malavolti and the *Mantellate* of Siena, T 61, *Letters*, 1:3. See Guy Bedouelle, "Mary Magdalene, the Apostle of the Apostles and the Order of Preachers," *Dominican Ashram* 18, no. 4 (1999): 157–177. See also Mary O'Driscoll, "Mary Magdalene and Catherine of Siena: Dominican Sisters," *Dominican Ashram* 15, no. 2 (1996): 51–60.

15. Letter to Monna Agnese Malavolti and the *Mantellate* of Siena, T 61, *Letters*, 1:4.

to assume—not in mere legend but in actual life—the role of a preacher in her own day.

2. Catherine's "Pulpit"

To those who knew her well, it must have been obvious that Catherine was a woman possessed by an almost uncontrollable desire to speak of the things of God.[16] But being a laywoman and not an ordained minister, how could she find a way to give tongue to her vision? Where in the medieval world was there a platform or a pulpit that would allow her to express the great revelations welling up within her? The answer to this question (and it is one provided by Catherine herself) is the unique and precious gift of authorship—the gift, in this case, of writing letters, either by hand or by dictation.

So filled to "bursting" was Catherine on occasion by the knowledge she received from God, she told Blessed Raymond, that "my heart felt as if it would break in two!"[17] But then she goes on to say that, "by his mercy," the Holy Spirit provided her with a way to "unburden" herself, first within the interior life of prayer, and second "in writing."[18]

> I was filled with wonder at myself and God's goodness when I thought of his mercy toward his human creatures and his overflowing providence toward me. He provided for my refreshment by giving me the ability to write—a consolation I've never known because of my ignorance—so that when I come

---

16. According to Raymond's account, Catherine would "have kept on talking of God, without bite or sup, for a hundred days and a hundred nights at a time, if only she had listeners who could keep following what she said and could share in the conversation" (*Life*, no. 62, 57).

17. Letter to Raymond, T 272, *Letters*, 2:505.

18. *Letters*, 2:505.

down from the heights I might have a little something to vent my heart, lest it burst.[19]

So engrossed was Catherine in the things she wanted to communicate, she had no time, as an author, to consider the niceties of form or style. Her concern was to be an apostle, not a genius. Nevertheless, it was precisely this passion for truth that, on occasion, set fire to her words, and transformed her into a writer of very considerable power. In the opinion of the Russian poet Boris Pasternak, when an author is "overwhelmed by what he or she has to say," then "the most extraordinary discoveries are made."[20] The Italian critic Giovanni Papini even goes so far as to claim that when Catherine of Siena was "inspired"—wholly possessed, that is, by what she wanted to say—"she succeeds, and without any special effort on her part, in equaling the greatest writers."[21] Such a high estimate of the work strikes me, as no doubt it will strike the majority of readers today, as exaggerated. But there are moments, wonderful to observe, when the suppressed energies of Catherine's thought explode onto the page with a succession of images and ideas, of words and perceptions, which appear almost to rival her own contemplative rapture.[22]

---

19. Whether or not Catherine learned to write by her own hand has been much discussed by scholars: see Catherine M. Mooney, "Wondrous Words: Catherine of Siena's Miraculous Reading and Writing according to the Early Sources," in *Catherine of Siena: The Creation of a Cult*, 263–287. See also Noffke, *Letters*, 2:505–506. On this question, Grazia Mangano Ragazzi writes: "On the one hand it cannot be ruled out that Catherine knew how to write, on the other hand there are no autograph writings in support of this claim" (*Obeying the Truth*, 25).

20. Boris Pasternak interviewed by Olga Carlisle in *Writers at Work: Interviews from The Paris Review*, ed. K. Dick (London: Penguin, 1972), 145.

21. Giovanni Papini, *Storia della letteratura italiana*, vol. 1 (Florence: Vallecchi, 1937), 432.

22. Note most especially the remarkable closing paragraphs of the *Dialogue*, the section beginning with the words "O eternal Trinity! O Godhead!" (*Dialogue*, no. 167, 364–366).

Catherine was a compulsive talker. One of the things she obviously enjoyed most in life was the opportunity "to speak of the marvelous things of God" with her friends and disciples.[23] Her hortatory style could be magnificent at times, but it could also on occasion be boring and repetitive. Once her imagination was quickened by a favorite theme such as the mystery of God's love in Christ, she was scarcely able to control the outpouring of her thoughts.

Writing to the Dominican Bartolomeo Dominici, and thinking of how in Christ we are clothed "in the fire of God's charity," she exclaims: "*Oh sweet love, charity, boundless delight!* . . . The Word has given himself as food, and the Father is a bed where the soul takes its rest. Love! Love! There isn't a thing we lack: a garment of fire against the cold, food against starvation, a bed against exhaustion. Fall, fall in love with God."[24] Catherine continues in this vein for a number of sentences, but finally she stops herself in mid-flow, confessing to her priest friend: "I don't want to say anymore, because I wouldn't stop until I died—or had bored you to death!"[25]

3. Preaching and Politics

Catherine's world was, like our own, marked by enormous change and upheaval, both within the Church and in society in general. An old world—the world of the Middle Ages—was disappearing fast, and what the future might bring was by no means clear. Catherine's contemporaries witnessed the damage caused by wars and by countless natural disasters, and they witnessed also the

---

23. Letter to Monna Alessa dei Saracini, T 277, *Letters*, 3:119.

24. Letter to Frate Bartolomeo Dominici, T 129, *Letters*, 1:234–235 (emphasis in original).

25. *Letters*, 1:236.

terrifying horror of the Black Death, a plague that succeeded in decimating almost two-thirds of Europe's population.

At the same time, a different kind of plague was at work within the Church: a plague of unbelievable corruption. With enormous sadness Catherine felt constrained to acknowledge that the Church she loved so deeply had become "a garden overgrown with putrid flowers,"[26] a bride whose "face is disfigured with leprosy."[27] "The mystic body of holy Church," she sensed with alarm, was "on the brink of ruin" unless God intervened quickly to help.[28] "Alas! Alas! Alas! My unfortunate soul! I see Christian religion lying dead. . . . I see that darkness has invaded the light."[29] Speaking to Pope Urban VI about certain corrupt "ministers of holy Church," Catherine has no hesitation in declaring: "They are more like lawyers who give off a filthy stench and a wretched example than like clerics or canons who ought to be flowers and mirrors of holiness." Accordingly, she exclaims: "At least, most holy father, let your holiness get rid of their disordered living, their wicked practices and habits. Please discipline them, your holiness, each according to his rank and according to what divine Goodness requires of him."[30]

In effect, Catherine is asking Pope Urban to act as Jesus did when, as recorded in the Gospel, he made "a whip of cords and drove out those who were selling and buying in the Temple."[31] The corrupt clergy of her own day Catherine describes as "filthy, greedy, avaricious dealers bloated with pride, who are selling and

---

26. *Il Dialogo*, CXXII, ed. G. Cavallini (Rome: Edizioni Cateriniane, 1968), 306.

27. *Il Dialogo*, XIV, ed. G. Cavallini (Rome: Edizioni Cateriniane, 1968), 37–38.

28. Letter to Niccolò di Romagna, T 78, *Letters*, 3:344.

29. Letter to Don Giovanni dale Celle, T 296, *Letters*, 2:535.

30. Letter to Pope Urban VI, T 305, *Letters*, 3:215.

31. Letter to Raymond of Capua, T 219, *Letters*, 2:91.

buying the graces and gifts of the Holy Spirit."[32] If not disciplined with an actual "whip of cords," then at the very least these corrupt men should be disciplined by some form of chastisement in order, as Catherine saw it, "to free them from their shameful disordered way of living."[33] Here, as so often in the life and writing of Catherine, we witness her urgent and unwavering concern to liberate people from bondage, in this case from the bondage of grave sin.

❀

When the Dominican Thomas Agni, a full century before Catherine, was commenting on the order's motto "To Praise, to Bless, to Preach," some of the complaints he voiced prefigured a number of Catherine's own anguished laments. He declared, for example, "*praise* has lapsed into silence, *blessing* has turned into insult . . . and *preaching* has made way for fighting."[34] The new world that confronted Catherine, both inside and outside the Church, was a world a lot more troubled than that of a century earlier. Now, more than ever before, there was need for courage and determination to work for peace.

As year followed year, and as Catherine's fame increased, she found herself being drawn into some of the most complicated affairs of the Church, and also into the murky drama of Italian politics. Viewed now in retrospect, her brief, dramatic life appears as a striking mixture of success and failure. Few of her attempts to bring peace between the warring factions in Italy were successful, her earnest plans and strategies betraying, on occasion, innocent naiveté rather than political astuteness.

---

32. Letter to Raymond of Capua, T 219, *Letters*, 2:91–92.
33. *Letters*, 2:92.
34. Thomas Agni of Lentini, "A Sermon on St. Dominic," in *Early Dominicans*, 62 (emphasis added).

But there were other occasions when Catherine was fully aware of "the political implications of her actions," when she knew very well "how to exert her influence in the service of her goals."[35] On the ecclesial front, for example, Catherine was not averse to employing tactics worthy of an astute politician when necessary. When attempting to persuade Pope Gregory XI to return to Rome from Avignon (at a time when many in Avignon were opposed to such a move), she wrote: "Let it please your holiness to hurry! Make use of a holy trick. I mean, let it look as if you are going to take a few more days, and then all of a sudden go!"[36]

Nowadays scholars are generally agreed that Catherine's political engagement was not, as earlier hagiographical readings of her career had suggested, "a mere backdrop to her saintly career."[37] Catherine needs to be seen not as "a mystic removed from the politics of her day"[38] but as someone actively engaged "at the center of the political and cultural movements of her time."[39] In the opinion of F. Thomas Luongo, Catherine's dramatic emergence into public life was due "to the political situation of the Church in Italy as well as to a culture that privileged female spirituality and prophetic speech."[40] I agree wholeheartedly that these two key factors should not be ignored. Nevertheless, the

---

35. See Blake Beattie, "Catherine of Siena and the Papacy," in *A Companion to Catherine of Siena*, 74; Piero Pajardi, *Caterina: La Santa della Politica* (Milan: Martello, 1993); Giuliana Cavallini, "Catherine and Politics," in *Catherine of Siena* (London: Geoffrey Chapman, 1998), 108–130; Carnea, *Libertà e politica in S. Caterina da Siena*.

36. Letter to Pope Gregory XI, T 231, *Letters*, 2:216.

37. See F. Thomas Luongo, "The Historical Reception of Catherine of Siena," in *A Companion to Catherine of Siena*, 24.

38. Luongo, *A Companion to Catherine of Siena*, 43.

39. Luongo, *A Companion to Catherine of Siena*, 45.

40. Luongo, *A Companion to Catherine of Siena*, 43. The "culture" to which Luongo refers did, on occasion, permit female ascetics and mystics to enjoy considerable acclaim, but those very same women were just as likely to meet with fierce and unrelenting opposition.

unique phenomenon of Catherine—the astonishing nature of her emergence onto the public stage—cannot, I believe, be explained by mere historical circumstances alone, whether cultural or political. What needs acknowledgment, first and last, is the unique and particular grace of Catherine's mystical encounter with God.

Mysticism is not much regarded by politicians who like to imagine that they at least are practical. But, according to Charles Péguy, they are mistaken: "They deceive themselves and they deceive others. It is the mystics who are practical, who do something, and it is they who are not, who do nothing."[41] Of course, that may sound like an all too easy and predictable romanticization of mystics and demonization of politicians. If, however, we consider someone like Catherine of Siena, and if we place alongside her, as it were, a number of the corrupt political and ecclesiastical figures of her time, the contrast may not perhaps appear quite so facile after all. According to Péguy, politicians "pillage" and "live as parasites," whereas mystics "build up resources" and "lay foundations."[42] I am inclined to think that there is more than a grain of truth in these remarks. "Mysticism may be laughed at by politics, but it is still mysticism in the end which nourishes politics."[43] Péguy believed that when institutions (political parties or religious movements) lose contact with their original source—their *mystique*—they start to lose their way, and harden into close-minded ideologies, groups totally self-focused and self-serving. That's why politics needs always to return to mysticism, to the source that nourishes.

---

41. Charles Péguy, "Notre jeunesse," *Cahiers de la Quinzaine*, XI, no. 12 (1910): 62.

42. Péguy, "Notre jeunesse," 62.

43. Péguy, "Notre jeunesse," 62.

4. A Word on Mysticism

There are, needless to say, many different kinds of mysticism. In his helpful work *Explorations in Theology*, Hans Urs von Balthasar contrasts the mysticism of someone like Catherine of Siena with that of the Carmelites John of the Cross and Teresa of Avila. Although both of these great Spanish mystics are Doctors of the Church, Balthasar makes bold to suggest that their mysticism was "not primarily a mysticism of service in the Church, but one of subjective experience."[44] "Mystical states," he notes, "are the objects of John of the Cross' and Teresa of Avila's descriptions."[45] And he concludes: "In this respect, Spanish mysticism is in strong contrast with that of the Bible," and "very different" also from "the dogmatic mysticism" of a saint such as Catherine of Siena, "with whom it was pre-eminently a question of serving the Church in conveying an objective message."[46]

Balthasar is attempting here to make distinctions that are certainly real but very difficult to express with accuracy and completeness. Although I accept the core of what he is saying, I am not convinced that he has expressed himself well. For example, little or nothing is said about the *ecclesial* significance and importance of the Carmelite tradition—the vital service, that is, given by these contemplatives to the Church at large. When Balthasar refers to "mystical states," he runs the risk, it seems to me, of presenting a false image of the teaching of John and Teresa. The fact that these two great Carmelites possessed an unmatched genius for describing the many and various "mystical states"

---

44. Hans Urs von Balthasar, *Explorations in Theology*, vol.1, *The Word Made Flesh* (San Francisco: Ignatius, 1989), 190.
45. Balthasar, *Word Made Flesh*, 1:190.
46. Balthasar, *Word Made Flesh*, 1:190–191.

experienced by contemplatives does not mean that the aim of their contemplation was to achieve some kind of inner psychological state of personal rapture. No; their primary aim, like that of St. Catherine, was to achieve intimate union with God.

That said, however, marked differences remain between the spiritualities of Catherine and these Carmelites. For a start, Catherine is out in the world, we can say, a fact that at once connects her way of life and preaching with the tradition of biblical spirituality. Also, whereas their work is filled with descriptions of the interior life, page after page of Catherine's work is filled with descriptions of the bewildering and scandalous condition of the Church to which she is so devoted.

For Catherine the supreme model of the contemplative life was Christ Jesus, "the gentle incarnate Word," whose "eye was fixed on nothing but his Father's honor and on realizing his desire for us, that we might experience God—which is why he created us."[47] To the Dominican Bartolomeo Dominici, she wrote: "I want you to imitate this Word who is our rule, and the saints who followed him. . . . I want you to be engulfed and set on fire in him, constantly gazing into the gentle fire of his charity."[48]

The "saints" whom Catherine has in mind here are two great biblical figures, one from the New Testament and one from the Old, one who followed after Christ and one who came before him: St. Paul and Moses.[49] In Catherine's understanding, their mysticism, at its highest point, does not end in a condition or state of private ecstasy. No—being set on fire with divine love, they become able and willing to sacrifice, if necessary, even their

---

47. Letter to Frate Bartolomeo Dominici, T 204, *Letters*, 2:80.
48. *Letters*, 2:80.
49. *Letters*, 2:80.

great contemplative privileges and joys for the sake of others. It is a mysticism of service.

"Imitate that dear Paul," she writes to Bartolomeo, drawing attention first of all to the wondrous rapture that St. Paul experienced: "It seems to me that Paul gazed into this eye [the eye of Christ Jesus] and lost himself in it."[50] But then Catherine goes on to say that, as a result of this experience, Paul was so transformed that he not only became willing to be "separated from God, an outcast, for the sake of his brothers and sisters," but that he actually longed for that condition. And St. Paul was not alone: "Moses, too, looked to the honor of God; this is why he wished to be cut out of the book of life rather than have the people die."[51] Catherine herself, with no less passion and urgency, exclaims to God the Father in the *Dialogue*: "What would it mean to me to have eternal life if death were the lot of your people?"[52]

Catherine, it's clear, could barely contain the longing she had to bring others to salvation. "Alas, sweet good Jesus," she exclaimed, "I am dying and cannot die. I am bursting and cannot burst with my longing for the renewal of holy Church, the honor of God, and the salvation of every creature."[53] The phrase Catherine uses there—"I am dying and cannot die"—is one that she repeats several times in her letters. Two hundred years later, the Carmelite mystic St. Teresa of Avila takes up the phrase once again, but uses it in a very different way from Catherine. True to her Carmelite vocation, Teresa's whole attention is fixed with deep longing on Christ her Spouse. Without him, the world holds little

---

50. Letter to Frate Bartolomeo Dominici, T 204, *Letters*, 2:80.
51. *Letters*, 2:80.
52. *Dialogue*, no. 13, 49.
53. Letter to Raymond of Capua, T 211, *I, Catherine*, 120.

or no interest. And so, in one of her poems, Teresa tells us that she is "dying" of great spiritual pain—because she cannot "die" physically as yet, and be one with Christ in heaven:

> Straining to leave this life of woe,
> With anguish sharp and deep I cry:
> *"I die because I do not die."*[54]

When Catherine uses the phrase, "I am dying and cannot die," she never uses it to express a desire to be out of this world. Of course, like Teresa, Catherine longs to be with Christ. But her passion for Christ compels her, as a Dominican, to want to serve the Body of Christ, the Church, here and now in the world, and in any way she can.[55] This is not to say that Teresa, the great contemplative, is in any way indifferent to the needs of the Church. Far from it. Like St. Catherine two centuries before her, she is possessed by the desire to see the Church of her time renewed and transformed. But Catherine, it's clear, can hardly bear to contemplate its reduced, unhappy state: "So much blood has been sucked out of her by wicked gluttons that she has gone pale all over."[56] Catherine is mightily frustrated. She longs to do more, much more, for "holy Church," no matter what the cost, but again and again she finds her way blocked by limitations of one kind or another.

> Alas, alas, my wretched soul! Would that I might never rest until
> I see a knife coming to pierce my throat for the honor of God, to

---

54. Teresa of Avila, "Poem – 1," in *The Complete Works of St Teresa of Avila*, vol. 3, ed. Allison Peers (London: Sheed and Ward, 1950), 278.

55. The sharp contrast indicated here between Teresa and Catherine in no way reflects the full ecclesial stature and great humanity of the Carmelite.

56. Letter to Pope Gregory XI, T 206, *I, Catherine*, 109.

pour out my blood into the mystical body of holy Church! Alas, alas, I am dying and cannot die.[57]

Hans Urs von Balthasar, when writing about Catherine, spoke of her particular brand of mysticism as "dogmatic," underlining the fact that, like the teaching of the early Church Fathers, the emphasis throughout is not on subjective psycho-spiritual states of soul but rather on an objective revealed message. What Balthasar says on this point cannot be denied, for the word "dogmatic" is unquestionably helpful. In order, however, really to capture Catherine's apostolic spirit, a lot more needs to be said. For what we are witnessing here is nothing less than dogma on fire: at the heart of the Church—indeed at the heart of the world—Catherine gives us a radiant and bold evangelical mysticism.

5. Letters to Two Popes

Catherine wrote to all kinds of people: cardinals, monks, family members, nuns, hermits, widows, priests, a mercenary soldier, a king, a tyrant, a queen, a prostitute, a lawyer, a poet, and— amazing to recall—two Roman pontiffs, Gregory XI and Urban VI. One scandal that had occasioned enormous distress under the pontificate of Gregory XI was that, instead of living close to his flock in the Diocese of Rome, Gregory resided at Avignon in France, continuing a long, drawn-out absence on the part of the Bishops of Rome. Catherine knew that this scandal had been the cause of untold harm to the Church and to society at large. Her

---

57. Letter to Raymond of Capua, T 226, *I, Catherine*, 172. Shortly before her death Catherine made the following prayer: "To you, eternal Father, I offer once again my life, poor as I am, for your dear bride. As often as it pleases your goodness, drag me out of this body and send me back again, each time with greater suffering than before, if only I may see the reform of this dear bride, holy Church" (Prayer 26, *Prayers*, 269).

letters to Pope Gregory, appealing to him to return to Rome, are memorable for the note of childlike warmth and intimacy in the way she addresses him, not hesitating now and again to call him "Daddy" (*babbo*).

But the letters are also notable for the peremptory tone adopted by Catherine. She presumes on occasion to speak to Pope Gregory more like a prophet than a girl-child: "Up, father, courageously! I tell you, you have no need to fear. But if you don't do as you should, you may well have reason to be afraid. It is your duty to come. So come! Come trustingly, without any fear at all."[58] And again: "Let us go quickly, my dear *babbo*, and fearlessly! If God is for you, no one will be against you. God himself will move you; God himself will be your guide, your helmsman, and your sailor."[59]

This letter was written in the summer of 1376. A mere six months later, much to Catherine's delight, the pope returned to Rome, and all seemed well. But there were enormous challenges ahead. One of the great ironies of Catherine's life is that the return of Pope Gregory to Rome helped to precipitate the tragedy of the Great Western Schism. After the death of Pope Gregory, with the election of a new pope, Urban VI, the Church found itself divided into two warring factions with two claimants to the Chair of Peter.[60] No event in ecclesial life could have wounded Catherine more deeply. It was a tragedy, one can say, that marked the few remaining years of her life. That said, however, Catherine never for a moment lost confidence in God's power to protect his Bride,

---

58. Letter to Pope Gregory XI, T 233, *Letters*, 2:213.

59. *Letters*, 2:217.

60. Pope Urban VI had wanted to lead a reform, but he was a difficult and impatient individual. Within a very short time he had so offended the cardinals who had elected him that they went back to Avignon in France, and there elected a new pope. Thus began the Great Western Schism.

the Church, from even the worst disasters. In a letter to Pope Urban VI, she wrote:

> There is nothing—no difficulty, no sort of trouble—that can overcome you. . . . The blows of wretched, wicked, self-centered people will not harm your soul's will. Nor will they topple holy Church, the bride; she cannot fail, because she is founded on the living Rock, Christ gentle Jesus.[61]

Commenting on the contribution made to the Church by people like St. Catherine, Pope Benedict XVI remarked: "How could we imagine the government of the Church without this contribution, which sometimes becomes very visible, such as when St. Hildegard criticized the Bishops, or when St. Bridget offered recommendations and St. Catherine of Siena obtained the return of the Popes to Rome?"[62] Catherine, on a number of different occasions, dared to criticize directly not one but two Roman pontiffs. After these clear and sharp communications, however, Catherine would always take care to strike a note of modest and quiet apology. Nevertheless, not for a moment does she think to go back on the unsparing message of truth she had delivered earlier. Yes, she makes her apology to the pope, and it is strong: "Forgive me," she writes, "most holy father, for all my foolish offense against God and against your holiness." But, then, with a freedom of spirit that startles, she declares: "Let truth, eternal Truth, be my excuse and my liberator."[63]

---

61. Letter to Pope Urban VI, T 306, *Letters*, 3:283.
62. Pope Benedict XVI, "Meeting with Members of the Roman Clergy" (March 2, 2006), no. 7.
63. Words addressed directly to Pope Gregory XI but included by Catherine in a letter to Raymond of Capua, T 267, *Letters*, 2:476.

6. Words Bold and Sharp

One of the things that made Catherine of Siena a great and compelling speaker was the gift she had for injecting into her discourse a bright, colloquial phrase or saying, a statement at once wholly unexpected and yet completely apt. To a man who was considering religious life but who was clearly finding it difficult to remain chaste, Catherine wrote urging him to free himself as quickly as possible from the world and its temptations: "All I ask of you and urge you is that you focus on freeing yourself quickly from the world. Give it a swift kick! For if you don't, it will soon enough be the one kicking you!"[64] Other no less strong and vivid phrases and passages can be found in page after page of the letters:

> God's love for us was so unspeakably crazy that, when we had become enemies because of our sin, God wanted to make us friends.[65]

> Open the door of your heart, for it is really rude to let God stand at the door of your soul without opening to him.[66]

> Do not be satisfied with little things for God expects big ones.[67]

> The coldness of our heart comes simply from our failure to consider how much we are loved by God.[68]

> They are really sad who let themselves die of cold when they could have the fire.[69]

---

64. Letter to Ser Antonio di Ciolo, *Letters*, T 44, 2:581.
65. Letter to Stefano Maconi, T 369, *Letters*, 4:338.
66. Letter to Stefano Maconi, T 205, *Letters*, 4:40.
67. Letter to Frate Bartolomeo Dominici and Frate Tommaso d'Antonio, T 127, *Le Lettere*, 2:229.
68. Letter to Ristoro Canigiani, T 279, *Letters*, 3:210.
69. Letter to Pietro di Giovanni Ventura, T 47, *Letters*, 4:14.

Now is the time . . . to seek the gentle God because he is supreme Goodness and is worthy of our love and searching.[70]

How big is our time? As big as a needle-point![71]

Let the dog of your conscience bark and gnaw when you consider that you have to give an account to God.[72]

Learn from the Master of truth, who preached virtue only after he had practiced it.[73]

If you would be the person you are meant to be, you could set fire to the whole of Italy![74]

When the devil finds the heart ablaze in the fire of divine charity, he doesn't come around much—no more than a fly comes near a boiling pot![75]

We need to get the teeth of our desire ready to chew hard moldy bread if necessary![76]

I long to lay down my blood and my life and empty my bones of their marrow in holy Church, even though I'm not worthy of it.[77]

Stones land only on those who throw them![78]

---

70. Letter to Three Widows of Naples, T 356, *Letters*, 4:291.

71. Letter to Marco Bindi, T 13, *Letters*, 4:20.

72. Letter to Certain Monasteries in Bologna, T 215, *Letters*, 3:12.

73. Letter to Raymond, T 226, *Letters*, 2:5.

74. Letter to Stefano Maconi, T 368, *Le Lettere*, 5:266.

75. Letter to Frate Niccolò di Nanni, T 287, *Le Lettere*, 4:214. Reading this particular sentence, it comes as no surprise to find Catherine, in another of her letters, making reference to what she calls "my free and blazing desire" (Letter to Raymond of Capua, T 371, *Letters*, 4:362).

76. Letter to Monna Caterina and Giovanna di Capo, T 118, *I, Catherine*, 163.

77. Letter to Pope Urban VI, T 306, *Letters*, 3:285.

78. Letter to a Woman in Florence, T 307, *Letters*, 3:322.

That last brief quotation gives expression to an idea often repeated by Catherine. When, as happened many times in her life, she found herself wounded by evil gossip or by calumny, she would feel an immediate pity for the perpetrators, knowing that, by their actions, they were (at the level of spirit) wounding themselves much more than they were wounding her. Thus, in a letter addressed to the Defenders of the Commune of Siena, Catherine remarks that some of her "fellow citizens" appear to be spending all their time speaking ill of her: "I'm sorry because the blows always fall back on the heads of those who deal them, since it is often they who are left with the guilt and suffering."[79]

The "stones" of opposition, the blows of calumny, must have been hard to bear all the same. Nevertheless, Catherine refused to give in to fear, refused to have her voice silenced. To Raymond she wrote: "We must proclaim the truth openly and generously, never letting fear silence us."[80] And, to a leading prelate whom she was encouraging to speak out in defense of truth, she wrote: "I beg you to act in such a way that First Truth's hard word of reproach will not be said of you: 'Cursed are you who were silent!' Alas! No more silence! Shout out with a hundred thousand tongues!"[81]

7. Preaching Judgment and Mercy

Among the most trenchant, most scathing letters ever composed by Catherine of Siena are a considerable number addressed to priests and high prelates of the Church. These men, far from possessing the integrity and purity demanded of ministers of the Gospel, were living scandalous lives. To one priest in particular, Biringhieri degli Arzocchi, a man who was not only

---

79. Letter to the Defenders of the Commune of Siena, T 123, *Letters*, 2:377.
80. Letter to Raymond, T 330, *Letters*, 4:43.
81. Letter to a Great Prelate, T 16, *Letters*, 2:117. See also T 115, 2:369.

corrupt himself but bent on leading others into corruption, Catherine writes:

> Oh, dearest father, give a little thought to your perilous state! In what great danger you are, drowning in this bitter sea of deadly sin! Don't we really believe that we must eventually come to the moment of death? Let's not doubt it: no one can escape it because of riches or rank![82]

At the very center of Catherine's thinking about heaven and hell, judgment and death, is the fact of human freedom. In the *Dialogue* she says of the divine Father: "Although he created us without our help, he will not save us without our help. He wants us to set our wills with full freedom to spending our time in true virtue."[83] Freedom, Catherine explains, has been regained for humanity "by the blood of God's Son," but human beings are still capable of stripping themselves of "the great dignity of reason and the life of grace and freedom."[84]

Alarmed on one occasion by discovering that Queen Giovanna of Naples, instead of setting her will to the defense of truth and freedom, had done the very opposite and surrendered to lies and falsehood, Catherine wrote: "No more of this for love of Christ crucified! In everything you are calling for divine judgment!"[85] That last statement of challenge is never, for Catherine, the final word. Almost at once, with genuine concern and kindness, she adds: "There is still time, dearest mother, to shield yourself from

---

82. Letter to Biringhieri degli Arzocchi, T 24, *Letters*, 2:156.
83. *Dialogue*, no. 23, 59–60. Compare this extract from Prayer 25: "You who made us will not save us without cooperation. For you who drew me out of yourself and made me without my help have not saved me today without my help. No, you have used my plea and my confession to free me from the bonds of my sins" (*Prayers*, 257).
84. Letter to Ristoro di Pietro Canigiani, T 299, *Letters*, 3:161–162.
85. Letter to Giovanna Queen of Naples, T 317, *Le Lettere*, 5:48.

God's judgment. . . . Acknowledge the evil you have done. . . . The truth will set you free from falsehood. It will dissolve all shadows and give you light and knowledge in God's mercy."[86] Then, moments later: "I long for your salvation with all that is within me and with all the energy of my soul."[87]

For Catherine salvation means, among other things, final liberation from the threat of hell, the threat of an eternal death. But it means also, speaking more positively, entry into the unimaginable joy of heaven. Both states of soul—eternal death and eternal life—are described with great vividness in the *Dialogue*. Catherine, one can say, is among the most notable preachers of what is commonly referred to as "the four last things": death, judgment, heaven, and hell.[88] Modern thinkers since the nineteenth century have tended to dismiss the last two—heaven and hell—as mere fictions. Karl Marx, for example, would certainly have had the doctrine of heaven in mind when he dismissed religion out of hand as "the opium of the people." The poet Czesław Miłosz, responding to that dismissal by Marx, draws our attention to another kind of drug that is being fed, he believes, to the masses in our own day. According to the Nobel Prize laureate, "A true opium for the people is a belief in nothingness after death—the huge solace of thinking that for our betrayals, greed, cowardice, murder, we are not going to be judged."[89]

I have no doubt that Catherine of Siena would have agreed wholeheartedly with Miłosz. If asked, however, to address the question of death and judgment in her own words, she would have

---

86. Letter to Giovanna, Queen of Naples, T 317, *Le Lettere*, 5:49.

87. *Le Lettere*, 5:49.

88. On Catherine's teaching on the four last things, see Suzanne Noffke, "Visions of Eternity," in *Catherine of Siena: Vision through a Distant Eye* (Collegeville, MN: Liturgical Press, 1996), 106–121.

89. Czesław Miłosz, *Roadside Dog* (New York: Farrar, Straus and Giroux, 1999), 20.

felt it necessary to speak first and last about the saving death of Christ Jesus, and about the way that our faults and betrayals can be forgiven by God before our own death. "This, then, is the way," she notes. "Reflect that there is no other path, that every road but this one leads to death. Along the way of Christ gentle Jesus death cannot assail us, rather it frees us from death."[90] But what of our sins and failures? At this point, Catherine challenges us to face, here and now, the judgment of conscience—not in despair but with confident hope in divine mercy. She writes: "Let us, then, for love of Christ crucified, pass judgment on ourselves in this life. Let us judge ourselves to be sinners, confessing that we have offended God. Let us ask for mercy, and God will grant it."[91]

Catherine's desire that no one should ever be lost finds its most daring expression in a few unforgettable prayers recorded by Blessed Raymond. To Christ, her divine Lord, she was heard to exclaim on more than one occasion: "Can I ever be content, Lord, that any one of those, created as I am myself in your own image and likeness, should slip through my hands and be lost?"[92] The answer that Catherine receives—an answer confided later to Raymond—is particularly strong: "Love of me," Christ declares, "cannot exist in hell, for that love would wipe hell out of existence."[93] Clearly struck by that last statement, that last image, Catherine makes bold to reply:

> If your truth and justice would permit it, I would love that hell should be wiped out; or, at least that no soul should ever go there again. And, if it were possible that, without losing love of you, I

---

90. Letter to the Curate of Casole and Others, T 3, *Letters,* 1:287.
91. *Letters,* 1:287.
92. *Life,* no. 15, 14.
93. *Life,* no. 15, 14.

could be set upon the mouth of hell to close it, and so prevent any further souls from entering it.[94]

The Father makes clear to Catherine in the *Dialogue* that the greatest mistake we can make in life is to imagine that human wretchedness is somehow greater than divine mercy. That conviction can all too easily lead to despair, and even to "the refusal, the scorning of mercy."[95] Over and over again we hear repeated in Catherine's writings the core message of the Gospel: "God's mercy (which we discover in the blood) is greater than our misery."[96]

> In the blood we discover the fountain of mercy. In the blood we discover clemency. In the blood we discover devotedness. In the blood our sins are brought to justice. In the blood mercy is satisfied. In the blood our hardness is melted. In the blood bitter things become sweet and heavy burdens light.[97]

For Catherine nothing in all of human history reveals the mercy of God more than the saving blood of Christ Jesus. Accordingly, when even the most inveterate sinner comes to the point of death, the blood poured out with such compassion can become a true refuge and a blessing. In the *Dialogue*, the Eternal Father, having in mind a sinner of that kind coming forward for judgment—in this case a priest—declares: "At the moment of death . . . you will not be able to take refuge in any virtue of yours,

---

94. *Life*, no. 15, 14. The compassion of Catherine is matched if not indeed surpassed by what was said of St. Dominic. One of the saint's companions, Brother Ventura, said of Dominic that his compassion extended "not only to the faithful, but also to pagans and unbelievers, and even the damned in hell, and he wept a great deal for them." This testimony was given at the Bologna canonization process: see *Acta canonizationis s. Dominici*, II, 132. See also Vladimir Koudelka, *Dominic*, trans. C. Fissler (London: Darton, Longman, and Todd, 1997), 122.

95. *Dialogue*, no. 37, 79.

96. Letter to Rainaldo da Capua, T 343, *Letters*, 4:269.

97. Letter to Don Pietro da Milano, T 315, *Letters*, 4:97–98.

because you have none."[98] That sounds like a decidedly final word. But what the Father says next alerts us to the startling nature of divine compassion. For, even at this most extreme moment of seeming hopelessness and despair, there remains for the naked, bewildered soul one last refuge, one last hope for salvation. And it is on the subject of this hope that the Father now speaks: "Your only refuge will be my mercy if you put your trust in that sweet blood whose minister you have been made. This [last refuge] will never be taken away from you or anyone else so long as you have the will to put your trust in the blood and in my mercy."[99]

This message is not intended in any way to encourage complacency or presumption. On the contrary, the statement of the Father that we hear in the next sentence strikes a note of clear warning: "Let no one be so foolhardy . . . as to wait for that moment."[100]

8. Preaching against Injustice

Almost one hundred of the letters of Catherine that have survived are addressed to civil officials and important political figures both inside and outside Italy. They contain passages that, in any age, would be remarkable to read. Catherine's language, especially when she chooses to focus attention on the brutal injustice being meted out to the poor in society, brings to mind at once the language of Old Testament prophecy. And yet the thrust of her teaching sounds again and again as fresh and immediate as today's

---

98. *Dialogue*, no. 129, 260.

99. *Dialogue*, no. 129, 260. Later in the same passage, referring once again to the "last moment" in the life of an inveterate sinner, the Father declares: "No one ought to despair. No, reach out trustingly for the blood, no matter what sins you have committed, for my mercy, which you receive in the blood, is incomparably greater than all the sins that have ever been committed in the world."

100. *Dialogue*, no. 129, 260.

headline news. Writing to civil leaders in society about leadership, Catherine laments that all too often rulers in the state, instead of being concerned for justice, "rob people of their honor, reputation, temporal possessions, and even life."[101] Instead of serving the people in their charge, they "look out only for themselves."[102] They have no scruple in allowing people of wealth and influence (who have been found guilty of some criminal offense) to go scot free. Addressing the governors of the city of Siena, Catherine writes: "I have often seen and continue to see guilt punished where there is no guilt, while those who are wicked and evil and deserving of a thousand deaths go unpunished."[103]

When decisions are made by leaders out of timidity or fear of what others will think, or because of bribes or flattery, justice in the state is very quickly undermined. Justice would also be undermined if it began to be enforced with excessive brutality. In Catherine's understanding, justice needs mercy, and mercy needs justice: "For if justice were without mercy it would be joined with the darkness of cruelty and would be injustice rather than justice. And mercy without justice would be like ointment on a wound that needs to be cauterized with fire. Ointment put on the wound without cauterization makes it fester rather than heal."[104] The image is rather startling, but it carries a necessary and profound truth. If the good of society is to be served, and individuals within society are to be protected, mercy must always be united with justice, and justice with mercy.

---

101. Letter to the Lord Defenders of the People and Commune of Siena, T 311, *Letters*, 4:308.

102. Letter to the Lord Defenders of the People and Commune of Siena, T 367, *Letters*, 4:321.

103. Letter to the Lord Defenders of the City of Siena, T 121, *Letters*, 2:414.

104. Letter to Pope Urban VI, T 291, *Letters*, 3:152. See also T 185, in which Catherine writes to Pope Gregory XI: "If a sore is not cauterized or excised when necessary, but only ointment is applied, not only will it not heal, but it will infect the whole [body], often fatally" (*Letters*, 1:245).

What, then, needs to take place if justice is to flourish in the body politic? First of all, according to Catherine, rulers need to "get rid of selfish love."[105] They need to overcome the attraction to "avarice" and "the desire for money or bribes."[106] And they need to stop trying "to please worldly folk."[107] If, however, such attractions and temptations are not overcome, justice cannot exist. Authorities in the state, swayed by greed and self-interest, will always be inclined to bring only the weak and defenseless to the bar of judgment. Catherine writes: "We often see such people exercising 'justice' only where the poor are concerned— really *injustice.* They act differently toward the great ones, those who can do something."[108] Afraid of losing their status, elected officials yield ground to the powerful. "But when they are dealing with the poor, who are of little account and whom they don't fear, they show a zeal for justice in the extreme, and without any compassion or mercy they load them with tremendous burdens for the smallest offense."[109]

What troubled Catherine in the legal and political world of her time, and must have also horrified her on occasion, was the spectacle of the rich and powerful in society ignoring completely the plight of the poor. Of such cold and uncaring individuals we read in the *Dialogue:* "They see a poor person, one of their members, sick and in need, and do not help. They refuse to give not only of their possessions but even a single word. Indeed they

---

105. Letter to Andreasso Cavalcabuoi, T 338, *Letters,* 4:82.

106. *Letters,* 4:83.

107. *Letters,* 4:83.

108. *Letters,* 4:83 (emphasis added). In a similar vein, writing to the civic leaders of Rome, Catherine says of certain men in authority who have become corrupt: "They aren't concerned about giving their neighbors justice except for their own selfish pleasure or to please other people, polluting justice and selling their neighbors' flesh" (Letter to the Standard-Bearers of Rome, T 349, *Letters,* 4:98).

109. Letter to the Elders, Consuls, and Gonfalonieri of Bologna, T 268, *Letters,* 3:97.

reproachfully and scornfully turn away. They have plenty of wealth, but they leave the poor to starve."[110]

Catherine was a witness to all of these things. Out in the streets and thoroughfares of Siena, she had for years devoted herself to the small and the weak, the sick and the needy. For her, therefore, it must have been an outrage to have to witness, day after day, year after year, poor men and women being brutally treated and cruelly ignored by the rich and powerful. Regarding those proud, unconscionable individuals who maltreat the weakest and poorest in society, the Father declares in the *Dialogue*: "They do not see that their wretched cruelty throws filth in my face, and that their filth reaches down even to the depths of hell."[111]

Catherine, in a letter to the Elders and Consuls of Bologna, remarks: "No matter where we turn we see people of every sort who are bereft of all virtue because of this evil garment of sensual selfishness."[112] Then she adds: "Look at the hierarchy!" With that brief, sudden imperative, Catherine was not, of course, suggesting that the hierarchy could be regarded as examples of holiness and unselfishness. On the contrary, she was pointing to them as appalling examples of exactly the opposite condition. While Catherine could be very sharp in her criticism of the secular leadership of her day, she was even more scathing in her criticism of the corruption of the clergy and the high Church officials. These men, ordained to the priesthood, were supposed to be living examples of goodness. Instead, Catherine laments, they "flourish in wretched, wicked vice—so much so that they spread stench through the whole world."[113] "Where," she asks, "are generosity of charity and concern for souls, where the division of their material

---

110. *Dialogue*, no. 148, 312.
111. *Dialogue*, no. 148, 312.
112. Letter to the Elders, Consuls, and Gonfalonieri of Bologna, T 268, *Letters*, 3:97.
113. Letter to Pope Urban VI, T 291, *Letters*, 3:153.

possessions to the poor?" In reality, far from helping the poor or defending them, these ministers "commit simony by buying benefices with gifts or flattery or bribes, with dissolute vain adornments—not like clerics but worse than layfolk."[114]

What impact did these sharp declarations concerning justice make on the secular and religious authorities of the time? The question, given the paucity of documentation of these rulers' responses to Catherine, is impossible to answer. But what burns like a flame across the centuries is the boldness of spirit—the passion for truth and freedom—that drove Catherine to alert the authorities of her time to the scandal of injustice in their midst, a scandal for which they were directly responsible. The challenge that Catherine addressed to both the secular and religious authorities sprang not from some abstract ideology but from an anguished concern for the many poor men and women who were suffering most. Catherine's words, sharp and revelatory when they were first heard, still sound today with hard and biting authority.

9. Courage, Joy, and Freedom

When truth or justice were being ignored, or were under attack, Catherine was obviously unable to hold herself back from speaking out. But when she found herself under *personal* attack—a victim of calumny and detraction—she chose to remain silent, making no defense. And she advised her friends and followers to do the same: "I mean," she wrote, "not to give any answer to anyone who tells you anything about me that to you seems less than good."[115] But Catherine then offers a further word of advice to the two

---

114. Letter to Pope Urban VI, T 291, *Letters*, 3:153.
115. Letter to Monna Orsa Usimbardi, T 93, *Letters*, 3:348. To another group of disciples, Catherine wrote: "You must patiently endure others' persecution and slander, defamation and rumor-mongering. You must suffer these things with genuine humility, not taking scandal or becoming impatient or raising your head against anyone" (T 214, *Letters*, 1:658–659).

friends to whom she was writing, advice that betrays not only a fine and radiant spirit of freedom but also great humor: "Here is how I want either of you to respond to anyone who talks to you about my faults: tell them they aren't telling you the half of what they could!"[116]

An enormous number of challenges confronted St. Catherine and her brave disciples. She speaks of "ridicule, torment, wrongs, insults, detraction, gossip, difficulties, and harassment from the world, from devils seen and unseen."[117] But no matter how many the trials facing her, or how cruel and imprisoning the circumstances surrounding her, Catherine always seemed possessed of an almost metaphysical optimism, a state of buoyancy and hope that, of course, was never achieved by ignoring all of the difficulties; on the contrary. Greatly distressed on one occasion by the gathering strength of the antipapal league, she wrote to a young, faithful disciple: "Now is the time to cry out. The time is ours because Christ's bride is being persecuted, by false and rotten members. But take courage because God will not scorn the tears and sweat and sighs poured out in his presence."[118] And then she adds: "My soul is jubilantly happy in this grief—because among the thorns I smell the fragrance of the rose about to open."[119]

Catherine, in both good times and bad, seemed always able to breathe an air of freedom and joy. "Cheer up," she wrote to two women friends, "and don't worry yourselves any more so that we may all be one in the fire of divine charity. That union won't be taken from us by the devil or by anyone else."[120] And to her great friend Blessed Raymond: "Be glad, father, celebrate! Without

---

116. Letter to Monna Orsa Usimbardi, T 93, *Letters*, 3:348.
117. Letter to Raymond, T 226, *Letters*, 2:6.
118. Letter to Matteo di Fazio dei Cenni, T 137, *Letters*, 1:182.
119. *Letters*, 1:182–183.
120. Letter to Monna Orsa Usimbardi, T 93, Letters, 3:348.

any slavish fear, take courage. Don't be afraid, no matter what has happened, no matter what you see coming."[121]

What, it needs to be asked, was the basis of Catherine's extraordinary hope and confidence? Why, in her letters, do we not find her distraught and disillusioned by what she sees happening in the world around her and in the Church? The answer to this question lies in Catherine's profound faith experience of God. Although not yet enjoying in its fullness the perspective of heaven, she already shares something of heaven's vision of earth as articulated in the *Dialogue.* Catherine understands that, even in our fallen, complicated world, God's name is praised and glorified. "True," the Father says to her, "the people of the world do not offer me glory in the way they ought by loving me above all things. But I for my part draw from them glory and praise for my name. . . . In all created things made for them I employ my mercy and love."[122]

Catherine, as is evident both in her life and in her work, was able to share to a remarkable degree in this generous and unexpected vision, and for one reason in particular. Over the years, in humble self-knowledge, she allowed herself to be greatly helped and encouraged by heaven's compassionate response to her own perceived struggles with temptation and weakness. Again and again, in her own understanding, she experienced "the high eternal Father" turning "the eye of his mercy" toward her.[123] And that no doubt helps explain why Catherine, the bright preacher of grace, finds that she is able to view the created world as God views it.

---

121. Letter to Raymond, T 211, *Letters,* 2:168.
122. *Dialogue,* no. 80, 150.
123. *Dialogue,* no. 135, 277.

Once, caught up in an ecstasy of prayer at Rome, Catherine was overheard to exclaim: "Oh Fire ever blazing! The soul who comes to know herself in you finds your greatness wherever she turns, even in the tiniest things, in people and in all created things, for in all of them she sees your power and wisdom and mercy."[124] It is, needless to say, because of this hope-filled, radiant vision of the world that Catherine's preaching is shot through with such manifest hope and joy. And it is for that reason also she can declare with confidence to her friend Blessed Raymond: "Be glad, father, celebrate!"[125]

That glad imperative from the fourteenth century finds a joyous echo in a reflection composed at the beginning of the twenty-first century by an English Dominican friar. Mulling over the meaning (for preaching today) of the Dominican motto "Laudare, Benedicere, Praedicare," Timothy Radcliffe makes the following wise observation:

> Becoming a preacher is more than learning to speak about God. It is discovering the art of praising and blessing all that is good. There is no preaching without celebration. We cannot preach unless we celebrate and praise the goodness of what God has made. Sometimes the preacher must confront and denounce injustice, but only so that life may have the victory over death, and resurrection over the tomb, and praise over accusation.[126]

---

124. Prayer 12, *Prayers*, 112. Addressing the Father in the *Dialogue*, Catherine exclaims: "By the light of understanding within your light I have tasted and seen your depth, eternal Trinity, and the beauty of your creation. . . . You, eternal Trinity, are the craftsman, and I your handiwork have come to know that you are in love with the beauty of what you have made" (*Dialogue*, no. 167, 365).

125. Letter to Raymond, T 211, *Letters*, 2:168. Again, to Raymond, and to some of his companions on another occasion, Catherine declares: "Love, love, love one another! Be glad, be jubilant!" (T 219, *Letters*, 2:91).

126. Timothy Radcliffe, "To Praise, to Bless, to Preach: The Mission of the Dominican Family," Manila 2000, *Informazioni Domenicane Internazionali* 388 (December 2000): 283. Radcliffe was Master of the Dominican order from 1992 to 2001.

10. A Preacher without a Title

At the time of St. Catherine, the term "preacher" was reserved for ordained ministers of the Word. Nevertheless, in one of her letters, we hear Catherine exhorting the layman, Sano di Marco, to "fight and *preach* like a man."[127] Catherine's followers, according to Suzanne Noffke, were not shy to speak of Catherine's "ministry" as itself a form of preaching.[128] But not all who knew her well in Siena shared the same enthusiasm. A contemporary of Catherine, the poet Bianco da Siena, clearly worried that public success might lead to "vainglory," and warned Catherine in one of his *Lauda* not to succumb to "the temptation of prophetic preaching" (*la tentazone del profetico sermone*).[129]

Blessed Raymond, although he never actually uses the word "praedicatio" (preaching) when referring to Catherine, recalls in his *Legenda* how "over and over again" he witnessed "a crowd of a thousand or more men and women . . . crowding in from the mountains and the country districts around Siena, just to see her and *hear* her."[130] What's more, according to Beverly Mayne Kienzle, Raymond "prefaces her apostolate with a careful progression of speech acts from childhood onward. . . . He uses graduating synonyms for the act of preaching, from giving words of edification and providing instruction to exhortation, until she is on her deathbed, when she delivers a 'sermon' (*sermonem*) to her *famiglia*."[131]

Although, at a popular level, Christian mystics are often viewed as men and women who possess an intimate knowledge

---

127. Letter to Sano di Maco, T 69, *Letters*, 1:67 (emphasis added). It's worth noting that the phrase "and preach" was eliminated by most copyists.

128. See *Letters*, 2:67, note 15.

129. A phrase from a *Lauda* by Bianco of Siena, cited by Eliana Corbari, "*Laude* for Catherine of Siena," in *A Companion to Catherine of Siena*, 237.

130. *Life*, no. 239, 227 (emphasis added).

131. Beverly Mayne Kienzle, "Catherine of Siena, Preaching, and Hagiography in Renaissance Tuscany," in *A Companion to Catherine of Siena*, 154.

of the higher states and stages of the spiritual life, they are not generally regarded as bold and dedicated preachers of the Gospel. That's why it will no doubt come as a surprise to some readers to learn that Catherine of Siena was one of the greatest preachers of the Good News in the entire Christian tradition. Present in her work there can be found, as one might expect, some truly vivid descriptions of her own contemplative union with God. But the principal concern of Catherine is not to speak of such experience, but rather to draw attention to the astonishing power and beauty of God's nature. That is her great theme—the core subject of the Good News—to which she returns again and again in her writings.

Towards the end of his *Legenda*, Raymond recalls one brief but unforgettable story. After St. Catherine's death, when her body was awaiting burial, huge crowds came to the church bringing their sick with them "in the hope of at least touching the hem of Catherine's garments."[132] Miracles were reported almost immediately and, as a result of the excitement that this provoked, "it was found impossible to take away her body for burial for three days."[133]

> During those three days so great was the throng that constantly filled the church that a certain Master in Sacred Theology, intending to preach a panegyric to the people on Catherine's virtue, and going up into the pulpit to do so, was altogether unable to make them keep still, and could get no one to listen to him. In the end he was heard by several people to say: "She has no need of any panegyric of mine. She is well able to preach herself and proclaim her own virtues."[134]

132. *Life*, no. 379, 351.
133. *Life*, no. 379, 351.
134. Life, no. 379, 351.

Well able to preach herself. Never was a truer word spoken regarding this remarkable young woman. Catherine of Siena was a preacher almost unparalleled in the Christian tradition. A woman without title or status, she became a prophet of unique importance for her age, a mystic who was not only on fire with the love of God but was possessed all her life by a passion for truth and freedom. At times she could, it's true, be decidedly intimidating. But at her core, there was always in Catherine's spirit "a joyousness, a sweet fire of love and light of the Holy Spirit, a heart brave and not fearful."[135] Fired by an unshakable regard for the beauty and dignity of the human person—and being unable, therefore, to bear the sad spectacle of men and women made slaves by the shadows of fear and oppression, of injustice and human weakness—this young medieval visionary proclaimed the Gospel of freedom like no other woman in history.

---

135. A phrase of Catherine's in a letter to the Carthusian monk Don Cristofano, T 335, *Letters,* 2:588.